ART STRUCTURE

A TEXTBOOK OF CREATIVE DESIGN

Moonlit Sail, by Albert P. Ryder

Art Structure

A TEXTBOOK OF CREATIVE DESIGN

by *Henry N. Rasmusen* *University of Texas*

With one hundred and fifty illustrations, including charts and diagrammatic drawings by the author

FIRST EDITION

McGRAW-HILL BOOK COMPANY, INC., 1950 • NEW YORK • TORONTO • LONDON

ART STRUCTURE

PREFACE

THE BLIND MEN AND THE ELEPHANT *

by John Godfrey Saxe

It was six men of Indostan
To learning much inclined,
Who went to see the Elephant
(Though all of them were blind),
That each by observation
Might satisfy his mind.

The first approached the Elephant,
And happening to fall
Against his broad and sturdy side,
At once began to bawl:
"God bless me! But the Elephant
Is very like a wall!"

The second, feeling of the tusk,
Cried, "Ho! What have we here
So very round and smooth and sharp?
To me 'tis mighty clear
This wonder of an Elephant
Is very like a spear!"

The third approached the animal,
And happening to take
The squirming trunk within his hands,
Thus boldly up and spake:
"I see," quoth he, "the Elephant
Is very like a snake!"

The fourth reached out his eager hand,
And felt about the knee.
"What most this wondrous beast is like
Is mighty plain," quoth he;
" 'Tis clear enough the Elephant
Is very like a tree!"

The fifth, who chanced to touch the ear
Said, "E'en the blindest man
Can tell what this resembles most;
Deny the fact who can,
This marvel of an Elephant
Is very like a fan!"

The sixth no sooner had begun
About the beast to grope,
Than, seizing on the swinging tail
That fell within his scope,
"I see," quoth he, "the Elephant
Is very like a rope!"

And so these men of Indostan
Disputed loud and long,
Each in his own opinion
Exceeding stiff and strong,
Though each was partly in the right,
And all were in the wrong!

* Reprinted courtesy Houghton Mifflin Company.

This book is the answer to a number of recurring questions concerning a criterion for art works put to the author by students and others over a period of years. There seemed to be a need for an outline and analysis of the basic means of the artist in the light of recent advances in the field, a clear and unified summary which would be practical as an art school, college, and high school text-book, or otherwise useful to anyone interested in the subject of art creativity.

Soon after embarking on the quest for a criterion it became apparent that a great deal of tolerance was necessary for arriving at a fair and complete outline as well as in teaching it. While the individual artist could perhaps indulge in a certain degree of intolerance and even find it advantageous in the pursuance of his own particular idiom, neither instructor nor student could afford to indulge in any such partly blind attitude. To get a complete picture it seemed that one would have to cast oneself in the role of a seventh blind man who, after groping from one part of the elephant named "Art" to another, comes to the conclusion that it is a queer and many-sided beast consisting of many parts and passions, each having its place in the over-all scheme of things.

In order to answer the question of a common denominator of quality in art works it was essential to take advantage of past advances as well as those of the present, and determine principles basic enough to be applicable to all types of creative activity, from ancient to modern and from abstract to realistic. To be truly liberal one would have to accept the point of view that there are various facets in both nature and man's reactions, and that no one type of art can tell the whole story or completely satisfy the individual or group expressive need.

The term *creative* was adopted as an over-all label, for it was broad enough to include all legitimate art forms, ancient or modern, yet by its very meaning would exclude the unauthentic. Within this creative field the term *unity* was found to be the primary criterion for evaluating relative quality in art works, and from this point on it was a matter of defining and analyzing the artists' means and the principles of unity and showing how the means could be molded into artistic form by the use of these principles.

An outline of these things might have been enough, but because of the prevalence of narrow-sightedness and confusion in the art field it seemed important to spend some time in clearing the air and in convincing the reader of the authenticity of the creative approach as against the imitative or noncreative, thus laying a solid psychological foundation upon which the creative powers could be developed. These subjects are taken up in the first and second chapters and in the conclusion of the book.

Another question to be considered was the proportion of reason and emotion to be prescribed for best results in creative activity. There can be no conclusive answer to this, of course, because it would never be exactly the same for each individual, and it would be hard to prove the exact degree of emotion or reason going into any given art creation. Beginning with the fact that human activity is normally performed with some sort of balanced ratio of thinking and feeling, one might say that this would apply to art activity in the same way and that the creator should use whatever degree of emotion at his command, controlled and perfected by all the intelligence and knowledge he may possess. With all the inhibitions accruing from our age of science and reason, however, most individuals are unable to make use of their emotions naturally and freely; so a great deal of emphasis should be placed on this aspect of the creative process in art teaching and learning.

In order to approach a clear analysis and presentation of basic art principles, copious use has been made of diagrams and charts throughout the book. While it is not exactly new, it is hoped that this enlarged usage will help the reader to grasp the ideas and principles at hand.

Let the author hasten to admit that conclusions arrived at from analyzing art works by such methods remain in the realm of personal opinion, for interpreting an art piece is no less an individual action than is creating one. It may also be kept in mind that in many cases there has been a purposeful exaggeration of structural details in order to better illustrate a point.

In arguing the advantages of such a method of art education, the author here states his agreement with those who feel that a work of art cannot be fully explained by this or any other method. In its most important aspect a work must speak directly to the spirit, must do something to the emotions of the beholder—something that simply cannot be explained by word, diagram, or any other means.

Art—like love, religion, and other emotional expressions of man—cannot be defined with any degree of finality, for after all the explainable principles are judged there remains much of the infinite, which is both illusive and impenetrable. The relationship of rhythms, forms, and passages that impress upon our senses a new spiritual experience is the significant quality of any of the arts.

A question often asked by art students upon being introduced to structural principles is "to what extent does the artist consciously use design devices in working out a given composition?" Perhaps few artists create a picture by actually starting with a pattern like the rhythmic line analysis of *The Three Red Horses* in Fig. 21 or any other such obvious method, but it is nevertheless true that all good creative artists to some extent know and use some such principle either consciously or subconsciously. How an artist goes about the problem is irrelevant, for no two do it exactly the same. The end result is the important thing.

It sometimes happens that an artist will feel so obsessed with an idea or mood that by merely spilling it out onto the canvas the theme will naturally fall into a design or form that is consistent and right. Actually this is the end to be striven for, and whatever the reasoning of the mind concerning design principles, it should take place either before or after the actual work on the picture—a charting of a general course to be followed with intuition, or a later perfecting of the design through intellectual reasoning.

The artist needs taste and feeling in organizing a work so that the finished result will show little trace of conscious labor or obvious rule. The theme must be intricately merged with design and application to express a mood or idea completely and forcefully, but subtly, and seemingly with ease.

Any expression becomes a work of art only when molded into a singleness by the principles of unity. That is the reason these principles have been made the subject of this book. They are almost the only rules that have any validity. The sooner the student can make these a part of his sensibilities the closer he is to becoming an artist.

So to the student the author would shout this advice: *Learn the rules well but learn them as soon as possible so as to get on to direct and genuine expression that is independent of all crutches—art books, this book, teachers, other art, other artists' vision—independent of all except that which comes from within Strive to attain a genuinely personal, creative, unified expression.*

To realize better such things as the complexities and variations of subjective expression and plastic design, the student must experience by direct contact the works of the masters, old and new; for words are less than adequate for interpreting the intricacies of plastic design, much less the meaning and emotion contained therein.

Apologies are offered to the many artists whose works are used for analysis. In most cases they are deserving of greater respect and consideration than is suggested by the mere diagraming of one or two isolated principles.

The terminology used in the book follows for the most part definitions found in Webster's Dictionary. Other than that, as far as possible terms which are most widely accepted are used. Where there seemed to be lack of agreement, or where usual terms seemed confusing, new ones were chosen or invented.

The practice problems are arranged from simple to complex, allowing the student to gain control and understanding of the subjects in a gradual manner.

Through open-minded experimentation with the ideas prescribed, each person may decide for himself the truth or error of the theory involved and either accept or reject it according to its ability to stand just trial.

Here may be set down the scientists' credo for truth searchers: "To accept nothing as absolute and final until by personal experience it is proved to be true and reject nothing as absolute and final until by personal experience it is proved to be false." To be of any use this credo implies an obligation to partake of lively thinking, doing, and experimenting, for if one is to accept or reject nothing except that which one proves or disproves, it is necessary to get busy and determine some conclusions. Until one does, an open mind must be retained.

The bibliographical list at the end of the book suggests the many sources from which ideas were gleaned for arriving at the outline herein presented. Of particular value were the works of Shelden Cheney, especially his book *Expressionism in Art*, and the writings and teaching methods of Ralph M. Pearson. While the essentials of this book had been formulated after several years of self-learning, experimenting, and teaching of the principles before meeting either of these men, the later contact with their ideas was influential in clarifying and pointing up the author's own. Another valuable source was Erle Loran's splendid book *Cézanne's Composition*. Mr. Loran graciously permitted the author to adapt certain diagrams from his book for use in the chapter on Volumes, Planes and the Total Means. For the chapter on Theme and Expression, ideas were suggested by the late C. Law Watkins in his exhibition, the Language of Design, held at the Phillips Memorial Gallery, 1940.

The author wishes to acknowledge his indebtedness to the many museums, galleries, artists, and others who were kind enough to furnish and grant permission to reproduce illustrational material used in the book.

Special thanks are due to the Metropolitan Museum of Art, the Frick Art Reference Library, the Whitney Museum of American Art, and the Museum of Modern Art, all in New York, for their cheerful assistance and cooperation in research and for the larger part of the photographic material used.

The author is grateful to Gail Martin and Marian Davis for their reading of the manuscript and their valuable suggestions for improving the form and substance of the text.

HENRY N. RASMUSEN

AUSTIN, TEX.
October, 1949

CONTENTS

1. THE CREATIVE ATTITUDE

Creative art, being based on freedom and originality, knows no boundaries except those inherent within itself and the limitations necessary to quality, which we label *unity*. It plays no favorites with styles or isms. It is a timeless gauge for measuring art of ancient, modern, or future days, including all significant, creative, and more or less unified human expressions of the material and spiritual world in which we live.

Actually the term creative art is redundant, because no expression is really art unless it is creative. But owing to the widespread ignorance concerning art and imitation, the term is used here as a label for the authentic as against the false.

To create is to select or invent elements significant to a given purpose and organize them into a new and unique form. It means originality. It means individuality. It means freedom of action. The opposites of creation in art are imitation, academicism, intellectual and emotional slavery. Creativeness depends on a certain attitude of mind. It is democracy in practice—an invitation to free thinking, exploration, and progression. Its opposite, imitation, spells conformity, reaction, and decadence.

Merely to set up a mirror to nature is not enough. To imitate is to transfer the object or view from one place to another. In doing this, nothing is said. Taking an image from one place and transplanting it (either all or in part) to another place neither communicates nor gives meaning. It merely says, "There it was; now it is here." It gives room neither for individuality, for organization, for expression of mood, nor for meaning.

As an index of surface facts, naturalistic imitation has its uses, as in anatomical charts for medicine, backdrop curtains for natural history exhibits, advertising illustrations, or even portrait painting. But to imitate nature or man-made works is not art, but a craft. It is possible that any of these things might be done in a creative, nonimitative manner and therefore be works of art. It depends solely on how it is done.

To be imitative requires no originality of thought or emotion, but merely practice in the craft of copying. It is the easy way. To be creative is the hard way (until the individual expressive powers are trained to work freely at least), but it is the only worth-while way. In it there are room and need for personal feeling, thought, and imagination.

The creative artist may use forms quite natural in appearance if he redesigns them, rearranges them, and gives them significance through selection, simplification, and organization (Fig. 2), or he may use nonobjective, abstract, or semiabstract forms to express inner moods, ideas, meanings, or abstruse beauties.

At this point we shall digress momentarily to make clear what we mean by the terms *naturalism*, *realism*, and *abstraction*. In Fig. 4 is outlined the traditional creative field, including three general categories—realism, abstraction, and nonobjectivism. Naturalism is shown outside this field because, being merely imitation, it is not a legitimate form to be used by the creative artist. Realism represents that kind of art which uses natural forms but modifies and reorders them to some more or less slight extent for purpose of design. At the other end of the scale is the term abstraction, which denotes a greater or nearly total departure from ordinary visual aspects of nature. By some the term abstract or abstraction is used to define the latter, as well as that art in which there are no conspicuous references to nature at all. In order to distinguish between the two degrees of abstraction we shall call the total-abstract kind of art *nonobjective*, which is not a perfect term but is probably the most often used of the several like ones, *nonfigurative*, *nonrepresentational*, and so on. At other times, when speaking of more or less abstract types of work generally, we shall use the word *abstraction*.

The areas covered by abstraction and realism are so wide that in order to be at all specific one needs to use a modifying adjective with the terms, as in the designations modified realism, designed realism, semiabstraction, near-abstraction, and so on.

In the chart we have divided the whole range into mathematical percentages, which should be as good a device as any for defining the degree of abstraction to be found in art works. If this method seems too

FIGURE 1. Still Life, by Peter Cammarata. Creative Realism. (Courtesy, Whitney Museum of American Art.)

arbitrary and technical for ordinary discourse, it should at least be helpful to instructors in designating problems wherein a certain degree of abstraction or realism is wanted.

To return to the subject of the creative attitude, the artist may interpret the obvious, outward, realistic aspect or meaning of things, or he may go deeper into the spiritual and emotional values which the eye alone cannot see (Fig. 3); but whichever he chooses to do, the work must be structurally organized. Whether realistic or abstract, the artist must clarify the expression of what he feels or knows about the subject by extracting certain significant things, recreating, dramatizing, simplifying, diagraming, and symbolizing.

The finished work must be judged on its own merits —on its own grounds, as a complete expression of an idea, mood, or abstract beauty as felt, seen, or imagined by an individual creator.

The following exact transcript from an early edition of Webster's dictionary perfectly sets down the attitude of the creative mind and suggests the need for such:

Imagination: The will working on the materials of memory; not satisfied with following the order prescribed by nature or suggested by accident it selects the parts of different conceptions or objects of memory, to form a whole more pleasing, more beautiful, more terrible or more awful than has ever been presented in the ordinary course of nature.

"But," we can hear someone say, "isn't nature perfect? Have we a need or a right to change its visual aspects for the purposes of art?"

Part of the answer is that nature is perfect only in basic principle, or in single units, but seldom in mass or from any one point of view. Where several forms are seen together, it is an exception when they are found to be in good geometrical relation one to another. So for reasons of unity, nature must be reorganized and rearranged, the principles of unity emphasized, dramatized, and exaggerated. Spacial contours must be changed to show variety, interest, and harmony in relation to other masses. Volumes and planes must be drawn out one from another by accentuated contrasts of light-dark and color, rearranged in space positions for reasons of delineation, harmonic relationship, and eye appeal. In this same way all the elements must be emphatically reordered and redesigned.

Furthermore, the outward physical aspect of nature is only *one* of the facets for artistic expression or interpretation. Decoration, expression of the inner spirit and emotions and of the subconscious, and expression of nonobjective beauties are some of the other divisions. As for the right to change natural visual aspects, man is more important than any other known

FIGURE 2. Young Hunter Hearing Call to Arms, by Marsden Hartley. (Collection, Carnegie Institute.)

part of nature, and he has the right—more, the duty to use nature in any way that serves a constructive purpose. At one time it was considered a sacrilege to tamper with nature at all. This right is seldom challenged any more in medical and other scientific practice. Nor should it be in the arts.

Many people, when introduced to creative art for the first time, are perplexed by the problem of distortion from the natural photographic norm, especially where the human figure is concerned. Somehow it seems to them less sinful or wrong to change the normal proportions of a tree, a hill, or a house, say, than a man. Admitting the need to distort or change the figure to some slight degree for purposes of design or expression, they wonder if there is not a point or line at which the artist must stop distorting, and just how far he should or should not go.

There are answers to this question. We may start by asking who is going to decide on such a line, and if the line were set, who else would agree with it. If a group of people who seem to be in agreement on such a point were shown works of varying degrees of abstraction by a number of different artists, it would be found that what seems to one a violation of the rule will be acceptable to someone else. If a limitation were set, even those who had made it would no doubt later regret it; for if they had developed at all in the meantime, their opinion would have changed, and the line of demarcation in their minds would have shifted. So we see that this problem is a personal one, and one that will vary over a period of time, even within an individual.

Another important answer is that if it were possible to come to an agreement, it would mean the end of freedom of expression. It would bind everyone into a middle-of-the-road position which would ensure only mediocrity and eventual stagnation.

Cultural values change just as surely as do religious or moral ones. The idea of women being more than a little immoral if they showed an ankle was taken seriously not too many years ago, even if it seems ridiculous to us now. Lines of limitation set up by the sanity-in-art people are every bit as narrow and shortsighted, as time will no doubt prove. So the sky must be the limit for artists as a whole, and for each individual the limitations depend on his self-chosen degree of artistic license.

Fortunate is he who possesses a liberal mind and can enjoy all types of creative expression, from designed realism to nonobjective design, accepting each form on its own terms, its own grounds.

FIGURE 3. Night Wind, by Charles Burchfield. A successful expression in the realm of fantasy. (Courtesy, A. Conger Goodyear-Photograph, Museum of Modern Art.)

There are people who, because of wrong training or environment, are actually aesthetic-blind where abstract beauty is concerned (really all beauty is an abstract thing) (see Fig. 7). They are able to enjoy only the literary or storytelling side of a work of art, in writing, painting, or music. There is nothing wrong with a story or sentiment, of course, if it is acknowledged as such, but where plastic beauty is concerned the theme is the shell, not the substance, of the thing.

It takes superhuman effort to cure oneself of this insensitiveness to the visual music in the plastic arts, and even with those not exactly blinded to it there is room for developing along this line. Practice in sensing is good for us all.

Man has an inborn tendency to draw away from new experiences and lie peacefully in the rut of his past. After the contour of his existence pattern is once set, he usually spends most of his efforts protecting and defending it against any change in its outlines. It is easier, more peaceful, and more secure to keep patching the old worn-out pieces than to admit of something else being better, and beginning anew.

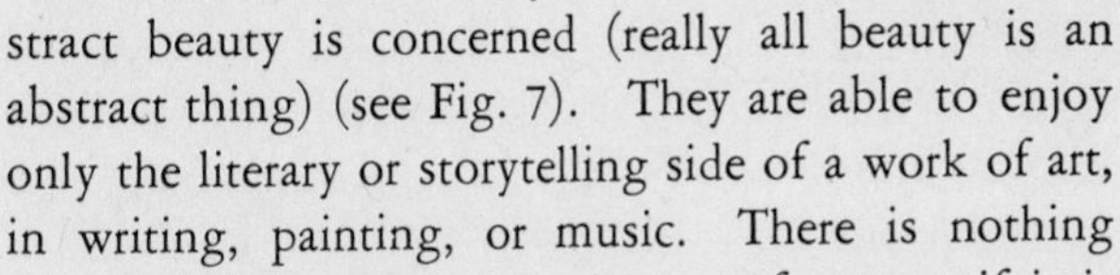

IMITATION
THE CREATIVE FIELD
Naturalism
Realism
Abstraction
Non-objectivism
0 1 25 50 75 99 100

FIGURE 4.

Time does march on. It moves past like a treadmill under our feet, and if we stand still we go backwards.

FIGURE 5.

FIGURE 6.

FIGURES 5 AND 6. Pierrot and Harlequin, by Pablo Picasso. Realistic and semiabstract drawings by the same artist. (Courtesy, Mrs. Charles P. Goodspeed.)

We must realize that progress means change, that the only direction for constructive achievement is forward. Psychologists tell us that the will to resist anything different from that with which we are already familiar comes from fear concerning our personal security. Because of this fear, change and progress usually take place under protest and opposition.

Pages and even whole books might be filled with lists of now-great men who, in their own time, were considered revolutionary and radical to the point of being dangerous or insane, or at best were scorned and neglected. Shining examples are Galileo, Columbus, Leonardo, Rembrandt, Edison, Wright, De Forest, Freud, Pasteur, Cézanne, and Wagner, to name a few.

We can be sure that many such men are living and working amidst opposition today, in our own time. Who are they? On what new problems are they working? These are questions to be answered only by those with open, searching minds. There is no greater thrill than taking part in a genuine progressive movement in any field in which one happens to be interested.

All the qualities suggested in this chapter—open-mindedness, imagination, courage, inventiveness, free thought, and progressiveness are attributes of the person with a creative attitude.

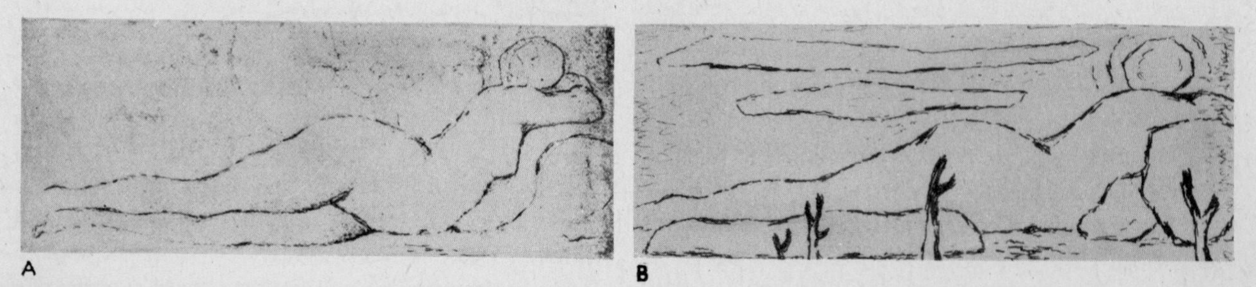

FIGURE 7. *Beauty is an abstract quality. A. Drawing of a reclining nude figure by Ingres. B. Landscape with hill, by the author, using practically the same outlines as found in A, showing that beauty is in the lines, not in the subject.*

2. THE ARTIST'S PROBLEM

Put in most simple terms, a work of art is an arrangement of symbols or units that expresses an idea, mood, or image. This means that the artist's problem is (1) to create units or symbols that represent his personal ideas or feelings and (2) to organize these units into a form that is vital and complete in its sum total. The quality of an art piece depends on the ability of its creator to express his thoughts and emotions with completeness and individuality.

In a few sentences, the creative artist's objectives might be outlined thus: He attempts to reproduce the outer and/or inner meaning or appearance of things, using individually conceived forms that are the products of his experience, feeling, or imagination, to express his aesthetic ideas and emotions in terms of the particular medium employed. He uses the design elements contained in plastic form in union with the artist's building materials—line, tone, space, color, subject matter, and craft to create a new and vital organism or entity of form. He uses emotional and intellectual freedom in organizing the subject or mood into a unified expression. He goes beyond composition in its academically accepted meaning, using design elements in organized interrelationships within a prescribed three-dimensional field. He respects the validity of the picture plane and the total field, realizing that the quality of his creation depends on the harmonious relation of all the elements staged within the walls of this defined plastic field.

To express means to give meaning, to say something. Men have always communicated with each other by way of signs or symbols. Ideas, moods, and meanings are translated and communicated from one mind to another only through this method. Drama, literature, music, sculpture, painting—all these are symbolical means of emotional and intellectual communication. Expressive body movements are symbolical signs; words in poem or story are symbols; musical tones are symbols; sculptural forms are symbols; the Morse code, a wink or a smile, an architectural plan, and the Ten Commandments—all are symbols that express emotions or ideas.

The plastic arts' language is made up of symbols which the artist creates from visual materials—lines, tones, patterns, and the like. These materials he must mold into a form that says something, either to the spirit or the mind, or to both. Although there is no such thing as an outline in nature, when we see a pure line drawing of objects, it signifies or expresses to us real objects in space, because we have learned to associate the symbol with the real thing. This same thing occurs in the use of words. Each different nationality associates a peculiar word or combination of words with certain meanings or ideas. Others not knowing the language find the symbols meaningless. People in the same way usually find a new art language foreign and meaningless until they take the pains to try to understand its symbolism.

Because of our habit of associating certain abstract symbols with real objects, we sometimes forget that the symbol is only a symbol and not the real thing. If someone happens to come along with a new symbol to replace the old one, we are disturbed because it upsets our notion of the reality of things and demands a mental reorientation.

In order for a student or artist to produce an individual work, he must originate symbols which best express his own personal feelings about the thing he sees or imagines. An apple, as expressed by Cézanne, is his own personal symbol of an apple. A hand or body by Michelangelo is individual and unique. So, to be personal, the expression must be the product of the artist's thoughts, emotions, and vision, being changed into personal symbols that represent these things.

Every person, because of differing heredity and environment, expresses things in an entirely unique and individual way—providing, of course, that he has not had this natural ability stymied or completely sapped through imitative teaching methods. This personal viewpoint must be honored, developed, and protected. It is lost through imitation of nature, imitation of other artists' work, or through imitation of period styles, be they old or new.

FIGURE 8. Hieroglyphics from wall in tomb of Har-em-hab, Egyptian. Ideas molded into pleasing visual symbols. (Collection, Metropolitan Museum of Art.)

The usual trend of the academic artist is to accept and imitate a style which has been safely dead for fifty or a hundred years. To one of this mind anything older is old-fashioned, anything newer is radical and a passing fad. On the other hand there are artists who are so intent on being up to date and progressive that they are blown from one new style to another like feathers in the wind.

Being progressive does not necessarily mean following the latest style. Progressiveness is a relative thing. In its true sense it means moving forward to something better than what we have had. So being truly progressive connotes a right-over-wrong moral attitude, a sincere wish to push on, to work and fight for whatever is found after careful deliberation to be most complete, most right, and most capable of expressing the artist's personal feelings and the mood and meaning of the present time in which he lives. Originality is best developed by learning basic principles, being naturally and simply oneself, and expressing things honestly, freely, and emotionally.

The role of the scientist is largely one of analysis; that of the artist, synthesis; yet, in order to learn to construct, the artist must also be analytical. The simplest of art works contains such a complex admixture of objective, nonobjective, and physical aspects that, in order to gain a more or less complete understanding, the whole must be broken down and studied in its several separate parts.

In a first consideration of a work of art we find that there are three main divisions: *form, theme, and technique.* In its biggest meaning form might be called the plastic structure, the inner and outer shape of an existing object. This would also apply to any single part as well as to a combination or group of units which go to make up the whole. In a painting, form is the resulting appearance of a combination of the quantities *line*, *tone*, *space*, and *color*.

Theme is the psychological aspect of the structure. It is the subject matter involved and the general idea, mood, or meaning to be communicated or expressed.

Technique is the physical structure—the craftsmanship or handling of materials for quality, permanency, and fitness to purpose.

In this book we are concerned almost exclusively with the problem of form—its character, its quantities, and qualities—mainly as they are related to the plastic and graphic arts, particularly painting in all media.

The essential quantities or means of form are, as noted before, line, tone, space, and color. We might add to these the secondary quantity, *texture*. Considering the quality of a form, we can say that a good work of art is one that has unity. A bad work of art is one that has disunity. Unity is the common denominator of masterpieces, ancient or modern, abstract or realistic. This points up the artist's designing problem simply and squarely as being the planning or organizing of the plastic means: lines, tones, spaces, textures, and colors, by using the basic principles of unity.

3. THE ARTIST'S MEANS

The builder of houses uses bricks and mortar, lumber and nails. The bricks and lumber are his means. The mortar and nails are the cohesive elements with which he holds the materials together. The bricks and boards are the quantities. The mortar and nails are the binding qualities. The quantities plus the unifying qualities equal the structural form—the whole. So that the end result may be more beautiful and more functional, the builder of houses uses a plan. The builder of anything needs a plan.

The true artist is a builder with a plan. His materials or quantities are lines and spaces, tones, colors, and textures. His binding elements or qualities are the principles of design—*opposition* and *transition*. The end result is *balance* and *cohesion*. Added results, which are refinements rather than basic principles, are *variation* and *dominance*. All of these together, depending on the success of the plan and its execution, equal unity.

FIGURE 9. Line and Structural Line. A. Illustrates lines of various characteristics. B. Illustrates principle of mass or structural line.

FIGURE 10. Fisherman, by Yasuo Kuniyoshi. A picture illustrating various line characteristics. (Collection, Museum of Modern Art.)

Line, tone, space, color, and texture, the aesthetic tools of painting, are also those of sculpture, architecture, interior decorating, and the other visual arts; although in some, one or more of the means is relatively minor in degree. For instance, in sculpture, color is of little importance compared to line, space, or tone. Even within each of the categories, every individual will place emphasis on certain of the measures, subordinating others to a minor role.

In a complete work of art the principles of unity are so interwoven, and there is such an interplay of the means, that the problem of theoretical isolation is a most complex one. For reasons of simplification, the problem of design in relation to a flat two-dimensional field will first be considered. Finally, in another chapter the third dimension, depth, will be added and the three dimensions analyzed as a whole.

In painting, the third dimension, depth, is actually an illusion. The artist's problem is to learn the characteristics of each of the means so that a relative depth illusion can be attained but at the same time completely controlled within all three dimensions.

Line, tone, space, color, and texture, each having certain differences and limitations as to character and dimension, work in different ways in relation to the laws of unity. In the following, the basic characteristics and dimensions of each of the means are considered.

LINE

Definition

(1) A linear or calligraphic mark. (2) A boundary limit of spaces, objects, masses, colors, or tones (structural line).

Dimensions

Length, direction, and general character.

Line can be thought of in two different ways as set down in the definition. In (1) it is an actual designated marking that shows certain attributes of character such as short, long, vertical, horizontal, straight, curved, wavy, and so on (Fig. 9*A*).

In (2) the line may be more imaginary than real, as in the contour line of a picket fence or the general lineal direction of a group of moving clouds (Fig. 9*B*). Defining it precisely as a general principle, it is a line, imaginary or real, that bounds two or more objects or masses of a composition. The former is an actual unit, whereas the latter is a line that defines masses or groups of units, spaces, tones, colors, or other details. The use of any of the means in creating form is in a sense an illusion, but this is probably more true of structural line than any of the others.

FIGURE 11. Design illustrating interesting two-dimensional closed patterns. Background shapes considered as an important part of the composition.

Calligraphy refers to the type of painting in which autographic lines or brush strokes play an important part in the design. Usually these are used in conjunction with color patterns in a more or less decorative, animated fashion. The Orientals used this stylistic idiom to good effect, especially the Chinese and Japanese, whose handwriting is of fine calligraphic design. Children have a natural tendency to express themselves calligraphically, especially in their early years (Fig. 110). Moderns like Cézanne, Dufy, Van Gogh, Marin, and Rouault make use of it, each in his own personal way.

SPACE PATTERN

Definition

(1) A two- or three-dimensional form, plane, or arid area. (2) A positive or negative area bounded by limits.

Dimensions

Length, width, depth, direction, and general character.

Besides having the same attributes of line (length, direction, and general character), space has two additional dimensions, width and depth, which set it distinctly apart from line. That is, spaces can have directional movement (horizontal, diagonal, upright, recessive, and so on); can have general characteristics, like wavy, straight, curved, and others; can be long or short; and, besides these dimensions, can possess width and depth, which endow them with possibilities of great variety in shape such as round, square, pointed, narrow, wide, flat, cubed, and many more.

The definition of space just given, it will be noted, covers all three dimensions, height, width, and depth. Accordingly, a flat shape or two-dimensional plane, as well as one of a cubic or three-dimensional character, could be called a space. Thus, both positive volumes as well as the negative areas or "air" between them could be called spaces.

For purposes of clarification it is better to separate the two-dimensional type of space from the three-dimensional. So hereafter a more or less flat two-dimensional plane or area (either positive or negative) will in most cases be referred to as a pattern. Even where a three-dimensional form is found, the spaces

FIGURE 12. The Artist's Studio, by Raoul Dufy. An example of open patterns combined with calligraphic line. (Collection, Phillips Memorial Gallery.)

that go to make up its two-dimensional plane surfaces will be called patterns.

Patterns can be classed as of two general types, open and closed. Closed patterns are those whose outer contours are more or less closed all around, making of them an isolated unit. Open patterns are those whose outer contours are open on one or more sides, being diffused and blended at the edges. This diffusion may be in tone value, color, or pattern.

Examples of closed patterns are to be found in the works of Brueghel (Fig. 116), Piero (Fig. 64), and Sassetta (Fig. 146). Examples of open patterns may be seen in the works of Dufy (Fig. 12) and Marin (Fig. 134).

Open patterns are often used in conjunction with some type of calligraphic line. Such a line acts more or less as a cohesive element in the form. Besides being an agent of decoration and delineation, the line sometimes follows the main pattern theme in a lagging, syncopated fashion.

A certain rhythmic variation in pattern contour may be found in natural forms such as the human figure, animals, trees, and mountains. A human limb, such as an arm or leg, or the whole body is seemingly symmetrical, yet on closer study it will be seen that there is much variety in the contour from one side to another. Where at a given point on one side there might be a convex curve, there will usually be found a concave one on the other (Fig. 50). The tendency of the human body is to fall into rhythmic positions, even in sleep.

This can be used as a rule for all drawing where variation in pattern contour is sought, rhythmically accenting the edges in relation to opposite sides, and each volume in relation to other figures and the frame.

In thinking of space in relation to a two-dimensional field, it is important to point out the negative areas or patterns left around the positive spaces or volumes in the picture. The same principles of design apply to the negative areas as to the positive ones.

TONE

Definition

The light-dark areas of a design. The opposites, black, white, and the range of gray values between.

Dimensions

Light-dark, length, width, direction, and general character.

It will be noted, as we go down the list of the several quantities or means, that each new one takes on the qualities of the one before it, besides having a distinguishing mark of its own. Tones in application take on the features of line and pattern and are integrated with them so that really they become one. It is impossible, for instance, to apply a light-dark spot to the canvas without its having the dimensions of length, width, direction, and other tokens of pattern and line. Besides the distinctive light-dark value in tone, there is the possibility of varied textural changes, such as rough, smooth, broken, spotted, and other surface effects.

While tonal qualities are necessary to the drawing of light and shade and chiaroscuro of a picture, it must be kept in mind that here we are considering only its decorative design possibilities in relation to a flat surface. This is sometimes referred to as *notan.*

Chiaroscuro refers to attainment of emphasis by using light-dark contrasts—spotting certain details of a picture—faces, hands, and other objects, and shadowing and obscuring other parts. This aspect of light-dark we consider under the heading Tone Dominance. Another aspect of light-dark usually considered under chiaroscuro is that of shading or drawing forms so as to give the illusion of three-dimensional reality. This aspect of the subject we consider in the section on planes and light and shade.

COLOR

Definition

The reflected visual rays of the light spectrum. One or more of the pigmentary primaries, red, blue, and yellow, or resulting combinations.

Dimensions

Hue, intensity, tone value, length, width, direction, and general character.

Color is seen to possess the qualities of all the other visual means of the artist, as well as hue and intensity, two distinct dimensions of its own. Hue refers to the chromatic position in the pure color scale such as red, orange, violet, and yellow-green, that is, any one of the three primaries or a combination of any two. Intensity refers to the color degree of a hue, its purity or modification toward a neutral gray.

FIGURE 13. Tone value chart, showing nine equal steps, including black and white.

FIGURE 14. *A twelve-color circle and diagrams of six common ways to achieve color harmony and balance. (Adapted from J. H. Bustanoby, Principles of Color and Color Mixing, McGraw-Hill. Courtesy, the author.)*

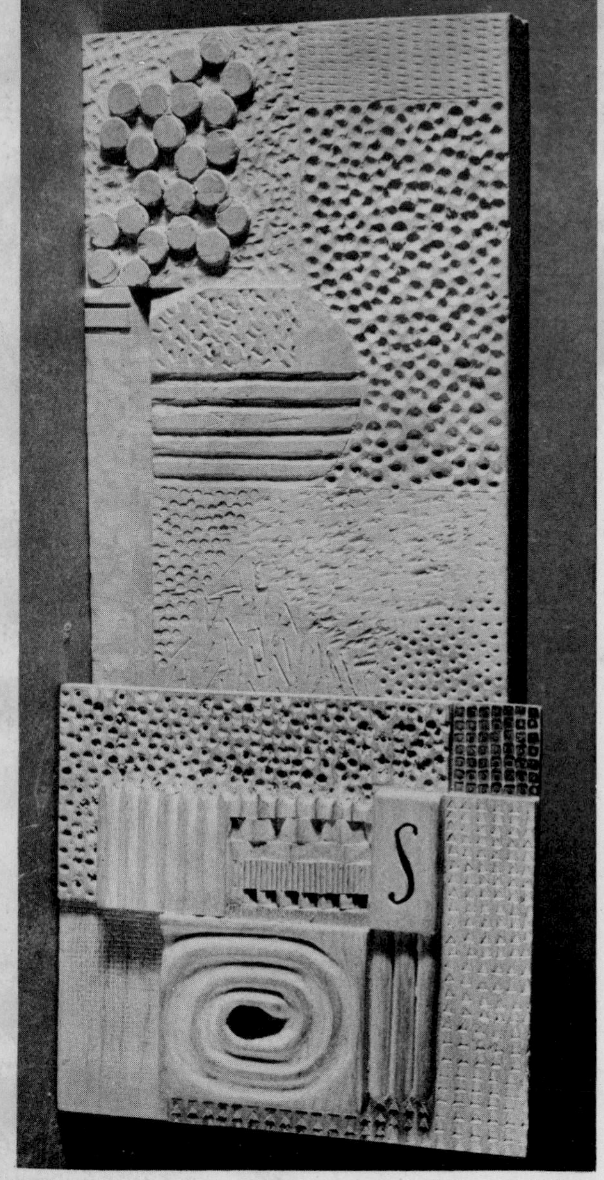

FIGURE 15. Surface treatment experiment by Margaret de Patta, former student, Institute of Design, Chicago. An illustration of various actual textures.

If one were to use color alone as the pictorial tool, it would be enough, for it is a composite of all the other means, with the possible exception of structural line, which, after all, is rather felt than seen.

The hue, intensity, and tone-value properties of color give it endless textural possibilities, to say nothing of an unlimited means for plastic (three-dimensional design) and expressive form (interpretation of ideas or moods).

TEXTURE

Definition

The actual or seeming tactile or touch value of a surface area.

Dimensions

General tactile characteristics.

For the painter's consideration, there are two general kinds of textures. One is actual and the other simulated. An actual texture is one that possesses real physical-touch values like sandpaper, wool, or glass (Fig. 15). A simulated or synthetic texture has little genuine tactile character but is made to seem so to the eye by decorative effects of color, pattern, tone, and line (Fig. 16).

Texture is not a basic means of form in itself but

FIGURE 16. Various simulated textures.

rather a result of the other means. For instance, its general tactile effects, such as smooth, rough, broken, spotted, and the rest, are arrived at by using the means of color, tone, pattern, and line contrasts and variations. However, for purposes of analysis, texture needs to be considered as an element on its own. As with the other means, texture possesses qualities of plastic, expressive, and decorative value for organizing or viewing a work of art.

Decoration is a term that is used often and one which we might here define. It is closely related to design, and by some the terms are used interchangeably. In our analysis we would limit the meaning of the word to describe an allover sensuous decorative effect as opposed to that which makes one area of the design more dominant, relegating others to a subordinate role. Decoration in this sense functions better where the essential flatness needs to be retained or where sensual and ornamental, rather than expressionistic or realistic, values are the aim, although these things to some extent must enter in. Repetition plays the largest role in decorative works. Repetition of similar patterns and colors tends to hold them to a limited extension into the third dimension, spreading them vertically and horizontally on a flat plane.

The tendency in contemporary art, especially in abstract works, is to eliminate any particular center of interest and spread the emphasis over the whole of the picture field, right to the frame edges. This coincides with the type of unity found in the universe as a whole in contrast to a focus on one central body, around which subordinate forms revolve. While this allover design lends decorative character to the form in a sense, the work could be called either decorative or expressive, depending on the emphasis placed on sensual or otherwise deeper values.

4. UNITY, THE UNIVERSAL LAW

Unity means oneness, a combination of parts so as to make a complete whole.

In nature we find the principle of unity a universal one. Countless groups of planets and nebulae together make up the universe—at once cohesive, balanced, and right. In each infinitesimal part, as well as in the incorporate mass, we find working the unifying principles that give form and order to spirit and matter, oneness to the whole. Complete in sum total, planetary systems and star clusters that make up the universe are in turn composed of smaller groups and units held together by laws of cohesion and balance—from big to little, from universe to atom.

The drama in design, as in life, results from creating unity out of chaos, reconciling the extremes, bringing opposites into agreement. This is done in effect by binding the opposites into a oneness through their offspring, the related or transitional units between these extremes. Considering the tonal contrasts of black and white, for instance, one or more tones of medium gray between would tend to reconcile the two by creating units common to both.

Another way of arriving at a unity of the two would be to repeat amounts of these contrasting black and white tones at various intervals across an area between them.

There seem to be two different means of balance in nature, one an equilibrium attained through the offsetting influences of contrasts, and the other a cohesive balance gained by the repetition of things alike. This paradoxical idea is seen in the male-female principle in life, and the possible unity of these opposites arriving out of common interests—offspring, common property, ideas, and ideals. It seems that no real unity is possible without some degree of both these principles, the like and the unlike. Even within

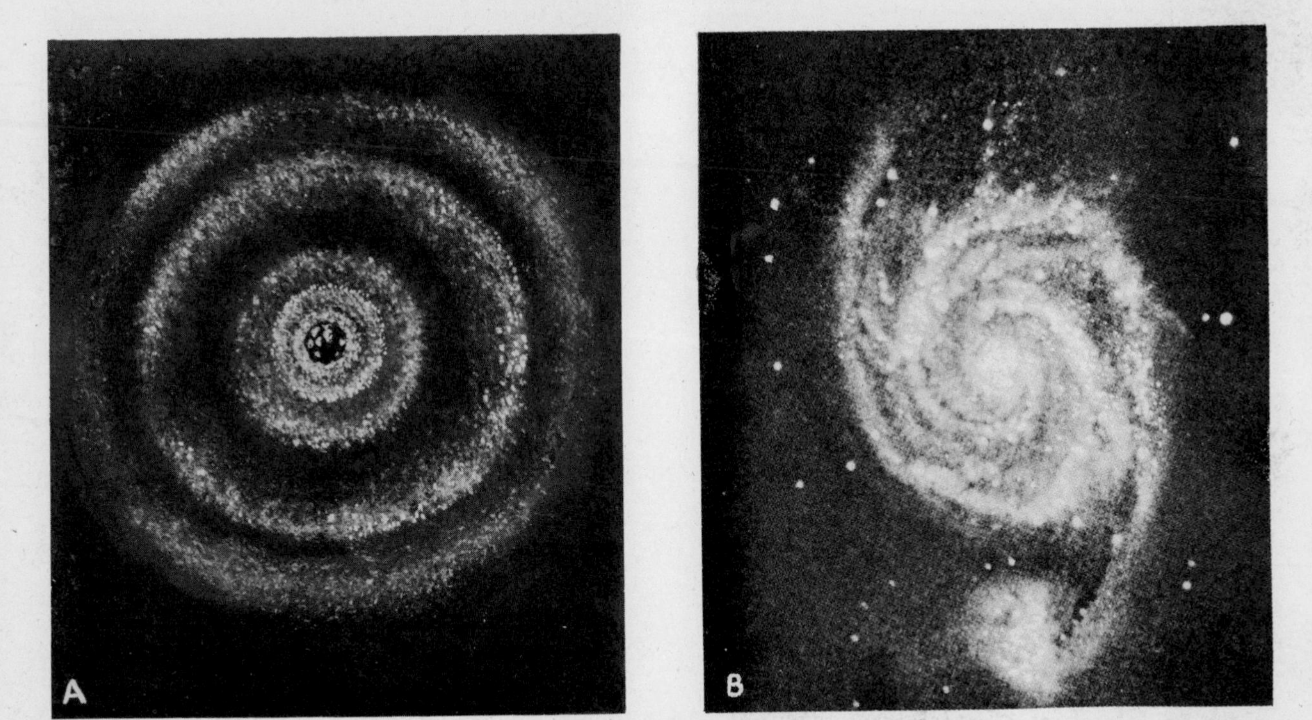

FIGURE 17. Unity, the universal law. A. Diagrammatic picture of an atom. The rings are orbits of whizzing electrons. B. Photograph of the great spiral nebula.

any single unit there can be found offsetting contrasts as well as harmonious principles that hold the conflicting ideas together.

It can perhaps be stated that a form is most vital and dramatic when the contrasts are more divergent. It follows that a less dramatic form is more stable but, by the same token, less striking.

Relatively speaking, where form is, there is unity. Where unity is, there is form. Where unity is not, there is formlessness and confusion.

The fluctuation resulting from the continuous construction-destruction, disintegration-integration process seems to animate things with movement, power, and life. This is the principle of transition.

The ends or extremities of all things in nature are necessarily complementary to each other and are usually seen to exist in the form of a positive and a negative. This is the principle of opposition.

Oppositions that set the extremities of the form also give balance. Transitional rhythms and repetitions between these ends lend consistence, and this natural play between the complementary forces results in dominance and variety. So opposition and transition are the fundamental laws. (In analyzing transition we find that it consists of rhythm and/or repetition.) Balance is the result of opposition. Cohesion is the result of transition. Variation and dominance are results of opposition and transition in combination.

Positive and negative elements that offset each other and fix the limits of things can be illustrated by noting the natural complementary forces of night and day, male and female, good and bad, sweet and sour, God and Satan, horizontal and vertical, black and white, and the rest.

Transitional sequences—related rhythms and reiterative passages between the extremities—give substance to the inner form, reconcile the opposites, and result in coherence of the whole. The principle of rhythm is shown in the harmonic sequences of the color, music, and tonal scales, of branches of trees, flow of water, grass in the wind, and many more.

The other means of transition, the principle of repetition, is seen in the duplication of characteristics in a species, heartbeats, symmetrical sides of the human body, a row of cathedral windows, and so on.

Dominance and variation, secondary but still important, are in nature the outcome of the normal workings of reconciliation.

The dominating feature that subordinates other units because of its contrary type is effected largely by being opposite in size, shape, color, or some other

THE ARTISTS MEANS + THE BASIC PRINCIPLES = FORM

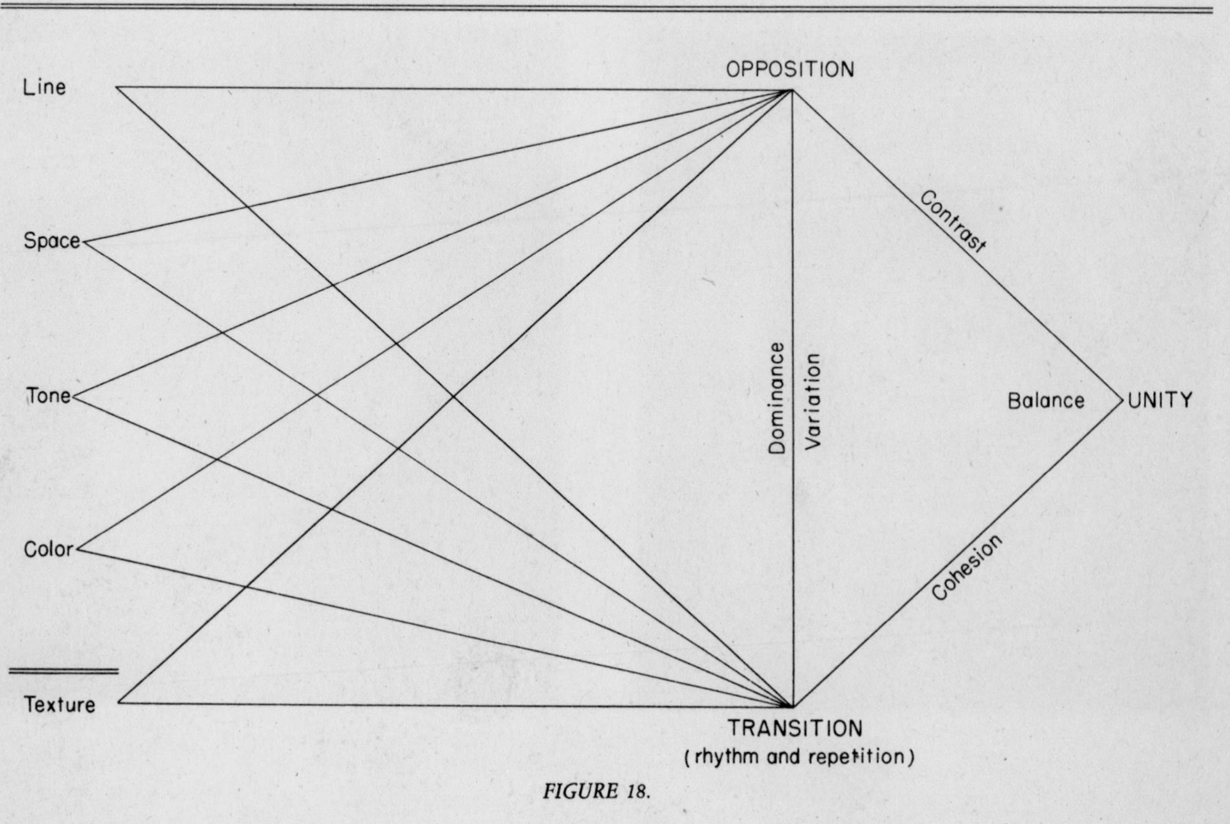

FIGURE 18.

characteristic, although transition sometimes gives emphasis by directional movements toward or away from this point of attraction.

A greater order of things is brought about by placing them in groups or masses. The human mind seems to demand this sort of classification for better comprehension. Some psychologists, studying our habits in thinking and remembering, say that the ability to remember things that are classified into groups is on the average twice as great as with objects not grouped or classified.

This principle of mass dominance is important to remember in relation to line, space, tone, color, and texture, as well as any other distinctive motifs that might be used in a design.

Variation, another result of opposites being reconciled, is important, not to unity, but to interest; for in variety there are diversity and change, the opposites of monotony, tiresome uniformity, and sameness.

An analysis of the dimensions and meaning of the structural tools, tone, line, color, space, and texture in Chap. 3 was important, because these are the aspects that must be considered in relation to the fundamental principles of unity suggested in this chapter. Our next problem is to define these basic laws and see how they work with each of the means.

5. UNITY OF THE MEANS

Definitions

Opposition: Contrary or contrasting. Radically different. Things that are opposite in character, direction, or place.

Transition: Passage from one place to another. Gradual change and reiteration by rhythms and repetitions.

Rhythm: Related movement. Analogous sequence.

Repetition: Duplication. Repeating something of same character two or more times.

Domination: Most outstanding feature. Center of attraction or interest. Grouping or massing of things into dominant units.

Variation: Deviation. Slight modification or change. Things that differ in some respects from a larger group to which they belong.

UNITY OF LINE

An offset balance or equilibrium is attained by playing complementary directions, lengths, and general characteristics of line against each other in a design. Upright against horizontal, short against long, curved against straight, thick against thin are illustrations of the rule.

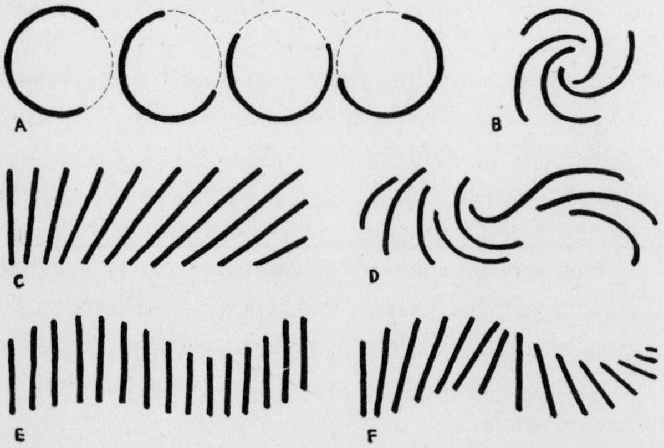

FIGURE 19. *Line rhythm. A. Diagram showing that line rhythm is based on the accented circle. B. The accents are combined to show rhythm. C. A sequence or rhythm of straight lines. D. A rhythm of curved lines. E. The principle of structural or mass contour rhythm. (Lines here are directionally repeated, not rhymed.) F. Line rhythm plus structural rhythm.*

Rhythmic line is of great importance in achieving cohesion and harmony of the various elements in a picture, and relating these to the format of the field in which they exist. It makes a consistent and dynamic relation and connection of parts that enables the eye to find its way through all the details of a design. Lines having a rhythmic change in direction across an area give the effect of plastic vitality and life, just as the rhythmic change of images on a moving picture screen at quick intervals gives the characters or objects movement and action.

Repetition of certain types and directions of line from one part of a picture to another is the other principle of unity which together with rhythm we call transition. The result of repetition of like lineal characteristics is to lend cohesion and balance.

FIGURE 20. *The Red Horses, by Franz Marc. Rhythmic line, tone and color are dominant here. (Courtesy, Paul E. Geier.)*

FIGURE 21. *Analysis of Figure 20. Horses, hills, ground, and shrubbery all unified into a oneness by structural line.*

FIGURE 22. Procession of Lord Maeda of Kaga, by Hishakawa Moronobu. (Collection, Art Institute of Chicago.)

Dominance is attained where line is concerned by using the laws of opposition and transition in an unusually strong degree at some point of the design, attracting attention to the area. For instance, when the rest of the design is generally harmonious and two lines at some point seem to clash or oppose each other in length, direction, or general character, they become the center of attraction. The dominant role played by these lines is strengthened when the eye is led toward the area by transitional passages of line and other means.

Unity and variety are acquired and strengthened when lines are massed or grouped together in certain areas of a design, leaving the other areas subordinate.

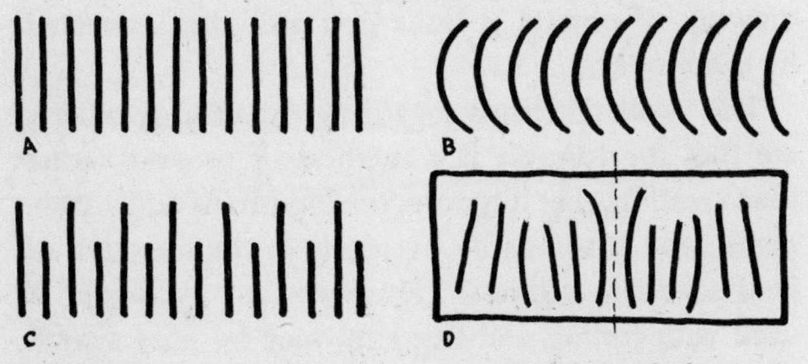

FIGURE 23. Line repetition. A. Diagram of straight lines. B. Repetition of curved lines. C. Repetition with variation of size. D. The basis of symmetrical balance (repetition of like forms on two sides of a central line).

UNITY OF PATTERN

Because *pattern* has the dimension of width besides those others it holds in common with line, an equipoise can be attained by contrasting wide patterns against narrow, large against small, round against square, complex against simple, and so on.

Harmonious pattern relationships such as a sequence of sizes, shapes, and types, as well as a repetition of certain like qualities through the picture field, help bind the separate parts into a balanced and cohesive whole.

The principle of repetition, as with rhythm, has an

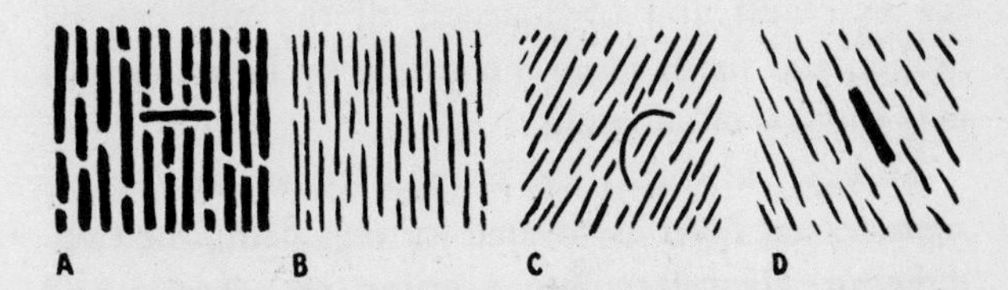

FIGURE 24. Line dominance. A. A line in opposing direction to others in a group will become the dominant attraction. B. A line becomes the dominant focal point when different in length. (The dominance is less pronounced here than with the other means.) C. A curved line becomes dominant when introduced among straight ones. D. A line becomes more dominant when greater in width.

FIGURE 25. Pour Jockey, by Joan Miro. Nursery Decor. (Collection, Pierre Matisse. Photograph, courtesy, Museum of Modern Art.)

effect of giving both cohesiveness and balance to a design. A relatedness results from repeating like patterns from certain parts of the picture in other areas; hence cohesion, and at the same time balance. This balancing of patterns from side to side of an imaginary central line or axis can be best illustrated by the principle of the counterbalance weighing machine. It is wise to remember that, although we are isolating each means for purposes of analysis, they are almost never found alone in a work. A good example of this is seen in this balance principle, where a heavy tone or color of a small pattern might equal or overbalance a larger one with weaker tone, color, or dynamic line (Fig. 26).

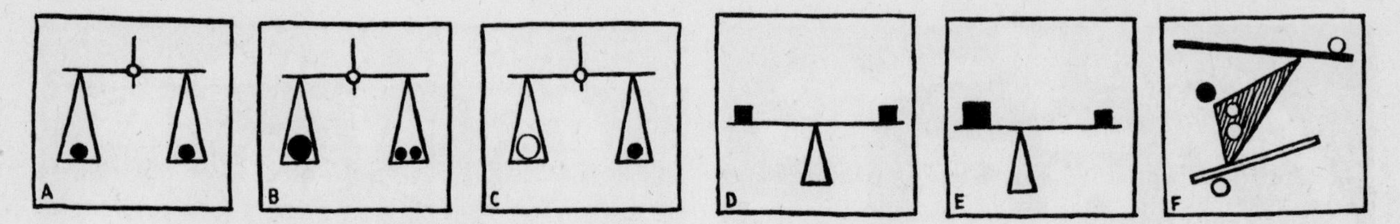

FIGURE 26. Diagrams showing the principle of balance, achieved by repetition of like or equal measures from side to side.

Where the principle of repetition is stressed above that of dominance in using space patterns or any of the other means, the result is to make an allover decorative effect, as against the subordination to a central interest plan.

When opposition, rhythm, and repetition are used, the exactness and obviousness of the rule can be broken and made more interesting by bringing into play the law of variation.

An exact mathematical formula known as *dynamic symmetry* has been discovered for organizing the two-dimensional surface into pleasing proportions and has been used advantageously by some artists.

Most art students have heard about the rule of dividing an area into odd proportions of 2 to 3 or 3 to 5 rather than in exact halves or other even relationships. Dynamic symmetry is the geometrical basis for deciding the outside proportions of a picture and dividing the surface design into pleasing space arrangements.

The system is based on the mathematical relationship of numbers called summation. In counting from one to ten, we add one digit to each number like this: 1, 2, 3, 4, 5, 6, 7, 8, 9, 10. When we say 2, 4, 6, 8, 10, we are adding two to each number. When we say 3, 6, 9, 12, we are adding three, and so on. If we say 1, 2, 3, 5, 8, 13, 21, 34, 55, and so on, we are adding the previous number to the last number given. This results in a rhythmic sequence of numbers and is the basis of dynamic symmetry.

In practice, a picture area is divided into good proportions by means of geometrical application of the rules of summation with compass and ruler rather than by arithmetical calculation, and the various objects of the theme are placed within these lines, or else the drawing of objects is done first and later corrected by these rules.

The usual criticisms regarding dynamic symmetry are that the formula is a method of proving rather than creating, that it ignores the important dimension, depth, and is too easily overdone in the direction of cold scientific stiffness. However, any such rule, if used with feeling and freedom, may be used advantageously.

Regardless of the means by which an artist arrives at a two-dimensional space organization, it is a fact that at the root of all good designs there is a harmonious geometrical relation of shapes and proportions. The beginning point is the given shape of the format or frame boundary itself. Each group or mass contour should be in harmonious relation to this shape and each subsequent detail in correct relation to the larger pattern shape in which it exists.

Aside from the importance of dividing the surface areas into pleasing proportions, there is a need for individual patterns to be varied and interesting in contour shape. While experimenting initially along this line, one might avoid obvious shapes like perfect circles, squares, triangles, and the like.

Subordination of secondary space patterns and forms is accomplished by using unusually large patterns at some vital place, or massing them in dominant groups which make others take subordinate positions in the design.

UNITY OF TONE

The limitations or extremities in the character of tone are fixed at the two ends by black and white. Between these two opposites can be charted a number of transitional tones of gray. While the limits of light-dark are set with black at one end and white at the other, any two or more tones on opposite sides of a medium value in the scale can be called complementary, and would create the balance so important to unity.

The use of any three or more tones in sequence between black and white would come under the law of rhythm. We say three or more because with only two there is no rhythmic movement or change. It takes three or more notes to comprise a chord. When there are only two units of anything, the eyes are equally attracted by each and merely jump back and forth from one to the other; but, when there are three, a transitional action begins to take place. This is true not only of tones, but of color and the other means as well.

The repetition of like tones in several areas of the picture helps the eye to take in all the parts and acts as an agent to tie all the sections together as one.

Other things being equal, a dominant tonal area—either light, dark, or neutral, as long as it is outstandingly different—becomes the feature of interest in

FIGURE 27. *FIGURE 28.*

FIGURES 27 and 28. Katchina Dance, by Emil Bisttram. Author's analysis shows the use of dynamic symmetry. Composition designed within three root fives, making free use of diagonals and intersections. (Courtesy, the artist.)

FIGURE 29. Space patterns cut from reproductions of pictures. A. From a Currier and Ives lithograph, titled Isabella. They are fairly interesting in shape, but there is a rather discordant or inharmonious relation between most of them as a group. B. From an abstract painting, Seated Woman, by Pablo Picasso. Here is fine variety in space shapes as well as group harmony. Spaces of this quality are bound to leave interesting background patterns even when set down with no thought of organization. Compare background spaces with those in A.

relation to the whole. By massing like or nearly like tones in certain areas of the design, a greater feeling of unity and coherence is attained, making the design more interesting and "readable."

Modification of the rigid laws of unity in relation to tone value is arrived at by the usual means of variation, making the creation more exciting, interesting, and attractive.

UNITY OF COLOR

To simplify the problem and avoid redundancy, we shall analyze only the distinctive marks of color and refer to the outline of the foregoing means for the other principles, because they are the same.

Within both of the distinguishing aspects of color —intensity and hue (besides light-dark which it shares with tone)—can be found complementary extremes

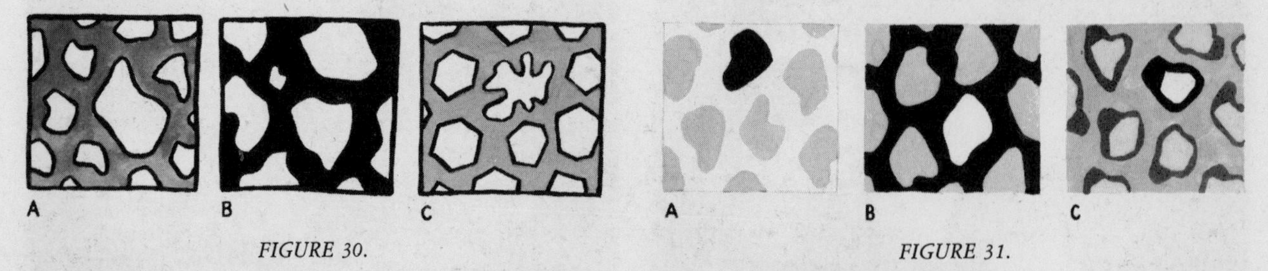

FIGURE 30. *FIGURE 31.*

FIGURE 30. Pattern dominance. A. A large pattern becomes the center of attraction when contrasted with smaller ones. B. A small pattern will attract the interest when placed among larger ones. C. A pattern becomes more dominant when of a different character from those about it.

FIGURE 31. Tone dominance. A. An area becomes more dominant when dark, in contrast to other areas which are medium and light. B. A light area attracts attention when contrasted to others which are medium and dark. C. An area of dark and light in combination becomes the focal point when played against medium or less contrasting tones.

necessary to the principle of opposition. In the pure primary color scale we know that the third color of the triad is complementary to a combination of the other two, so that if the scale were equally divided into six, twelve, or twenty-four hues, any two colors exactly opposite each other in the scale would be perfect complements.

In the case of intensity, the extremes are found to be a most intensely pure color at one end, and at the other a near or neutral gray. So it can readily be seen that balance is attained by contrasting hue against complementary hue, such as yellow against violet, vermilion against blue, and contrasting brilliant color against more neutral gray. With any of the means, including color, one need not always baldly use exact complements, for art depends less on mathematical exactions and more on approximates of the rule.

Between the two extremes found in both hue and intensity are found the scales of related or analogous colors and degrees which make possible the play of color chords, passages, and transitions so necessary to a unified form.

Strong contrasts of hue or intensity at some point develop a center of interest, just as do contrasting tones, spaces, or lines. A dominant allover color, pervading and modifying all other colors in the picture, sometimes gives greater unity to the design by relating all the masses and giving them something in common. This works also with line, tone, and pattern, adding the principle of domination to the en-

FIGURE 32. Mrs. Ebenezer Storer, by John S. Copley. Dominant focal point gained by contrasting light tones on dark background. (Collection, Metropolitan Museum of Art.)

FIGURE 33. The Lawyers, by Honoré Daumier. Dominance attained through contrasting dark tones against a light background. (Collection, Phillips Memorial Gallery.)

FIGURE 34. Italiope, by Aronzo Gasparo. Simulated textures used to add variety and surface refinement. (Collection, Museum of Modern Art.)

tirety and distinguishing it with unity and character. This principle we might call mass or structural color, tone, space, or line. Certain areas of an informal design such as a picture should be massed in like or related colors, giving emphasis in these sections.

Along this same line, a picture is usually more interesting and unified when either warm or cool color is used in greater degree—where one is dominant in the picture. This same thing goes for hue, intensity, tone value, and the other means also.

In regard to repetition, the same unifying principle is achieved by repeating certain colors and intensities through the composition in the same way as outlined for the other quantities or means.

Variation, working subordinately with opposition and transition of color, alters, refines, and enriches the ensemble; it makes it less obviously the result of rules, more attractive, diverse, and interesting.

UNITY OF TEXTURE

Concerning texture, unity is attained by the usual complementary and transitional laws in conjunction with the general character of the picture. Textures alike in make-up repeated; different kinds opposed; related kinds used in rhythm, some dominant, others subordinate; the use of rule marked by taste, variety, and freedom—all together make for tactile order, character, and interest.

6. THE THIRD DIMENSION

Up to now we have been discussing the two flat surface dimensions of the picture field only, the vertical and horizontal. Actually there can be no perfectly flat surface, visually speaking (outside a completely blank field), but only a relatively flat one, because the application of even the slightest line or color sets up a form-background relationship that gives the illusion of some degree of recessional space. In some types of work, of course, the recession is extremely shallow, like thin cardboards or papers applied one over another, but the depth dimension, however slight, is there.

The early Egyptian, Chinese, and Persian artists used a relatively flat type of form, and more recently many moderns like Gauguin, Matisse, and Braque have returned to it on the theory that the essentially flat character of the canvas should not be violated.

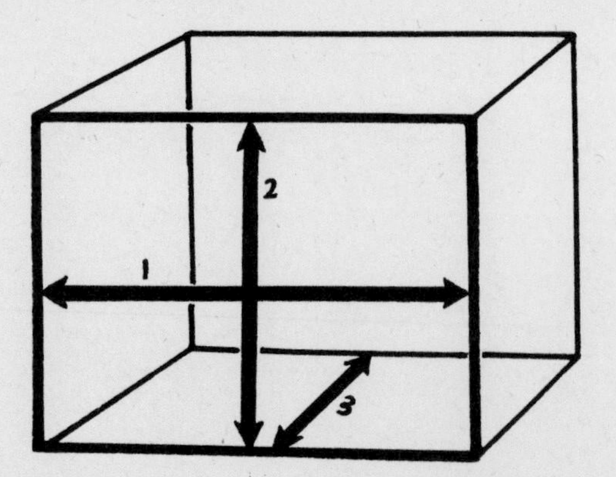

FIGURE 35. Diagram of picture field. The heavy lines represent the two-dimensional picture plane, the arrows describing the width (1), and the height (2). Arrow (3) shows the third dimension, depth.

Contrasted to their pictures are the strongly recessed works of Rubens, Michelangelo, Rembrandt, the contemporary Siqueiros, and others. The two types of form might be compared to the bas-relief and full round forms of sculpture. The preference for one type over another is largely a matter of personal like or dislike aside from the need to consider its fitness for the purpose for which the design is to be used. A mural, for instance, covering a large area should be relatively two-dimensional. The expressionistic and realistic approaches seem more appropriately combined with a heavier or more deeply recessed form, while the decorative, abstract, and nonobjective viewpoints seem to call for a shallower, two-dimensional one. Aside from these considerations, the plastic quality of any work must be judged according to the laws of unity and vitality in relation to the picture field set up. Whether one chooses to use either the shallow or deep type of form, there should be consistency in the approach and a balance and coordination of all the elements in relation to the total three-dimensional field decided upon. Also in order to hold the inviolate character of the flat picture plane, *volumes and planes should be arranged in positions dominantly parallel to the picture plane.* This is very important.

It is judicious to sense the difference between the two-dimensional and three-dimensional aspects of form and approach each on its own terms. For instance, when working with three-dimensional volumes, they should be manipulated and arranged in depth-space as though one were handling blocky sculptural forms made of clay or stone. When working with flat two-dimensional forms, the attitude would be different and greater emphasis placed on outline drawing and exterior edges.

To attempt to explore and expound the plastic ways and means of the third dimension by the written or spoken word is even more complex and harder to achieve than with the other two dimensions, and one must continually place more emphasis on diagram and illustration for explanation of the various points.

The arrangement of objects between the front and back extremities of the three-dimensional field is commonly known as perspective. For purposes of clarification and to get to the root of the problem we call the various points between the front and back, *distance planes*, so as to distinguish them from *directional planes*, about which we will say more later.

Distance planes are created and ordered mostly by relationships of size and intensity. As the size and intensity are modified, the object seems to recede to a more distant place. These places we call planes, like front plane, middle plane, and back plane, or foreground, middle ground, and background. Strong tones like black and white, warm hues like yellow and red, brilliant colors, and strong textures—all seem to take advanced positions near the picture plane. As they become more neutralized in character or strength, they take a more receding position. A knowledge of these factors is necessary to the artist in achieving three-dimensional design.

Every volume, color, tone, line, space, or texture, depending on its character in relation to the other means, possesses certain plastic receding-advancing qualities which are important in molding the picture into a unified and energetic form. The observer's eye is controlled and led through various parts of the picture at the artist's will, to carry over to the observer the mood, theme, or effect that the artist hopes to express.

FIGURE 36. Gas House District, by Niles Spencer. A painting showing strong three-dimensional planes. (Courtesy, Downtown Gallery.)

Ordinarily, we visually perceive forms in nature in two different ways, the *kinesthetic* and the *stereoscopic*. In the kinesthetic, we come to a realization of a given object by a series of eye movements around and across it. Objects close to the eye require greater eye movement than those in the distance because of convergence of the line of vision toward a perspective point, so that we instinctively conclude the distance position of an object by the relative number of eye movements necessary to take it all in. Close objects take more, far ones less.

Incidentally, we should remember that perspective is the result of the physical make-up and action of the human eye, and something that actually is nonexistent in nature. Lines do not really converge in the distance nor objects become smaller—it only seems so, because our own vision converges at a distant point.

Stereoscopic vision consists in the ability to see objects from two points of view at the same time. Having two eyes set at certain distances apart, we are able to see, to some extent, two sides of an object at once, and that ability gives a greater three-dimensional reality to the form. As things are seen from more distant points, this ability to see two views at the same time diminishes (again because of the line of vision converging in the distance), so that our realization of distance and three-dimensional form is enlarged by this stereoscopic factor of sight, depending on the relative displacement of objects from side to side and front to back.

Because of the natural one-view character of the flat canvas, it was formerly considered impossible to make use of the stereoscopic principle in painting, but modern artists, like Picasso, Braque, and others, have overcome this by showing two or more sides of objects and figures in one design, thus discrediting the importance of ordinary optics for the sake of greater three-dimensional truth-reality.

As for the kinesthetic, the artist may develop in his design the impression of pictorial movement by exaggerating transitional rhythms and repetitions

FIGURE 37. Study, by Michelangelo. Strong three-dimensional form produced by overlapping lines. (Collection, British Museum.)

FIGURE 38. Winter Landscape, by Hsia Knei, Ming Dynasty. An illustration of movement gained and controlled by use of overlapping pattern and accented line. (Collection, Art Institute of Chicago.)

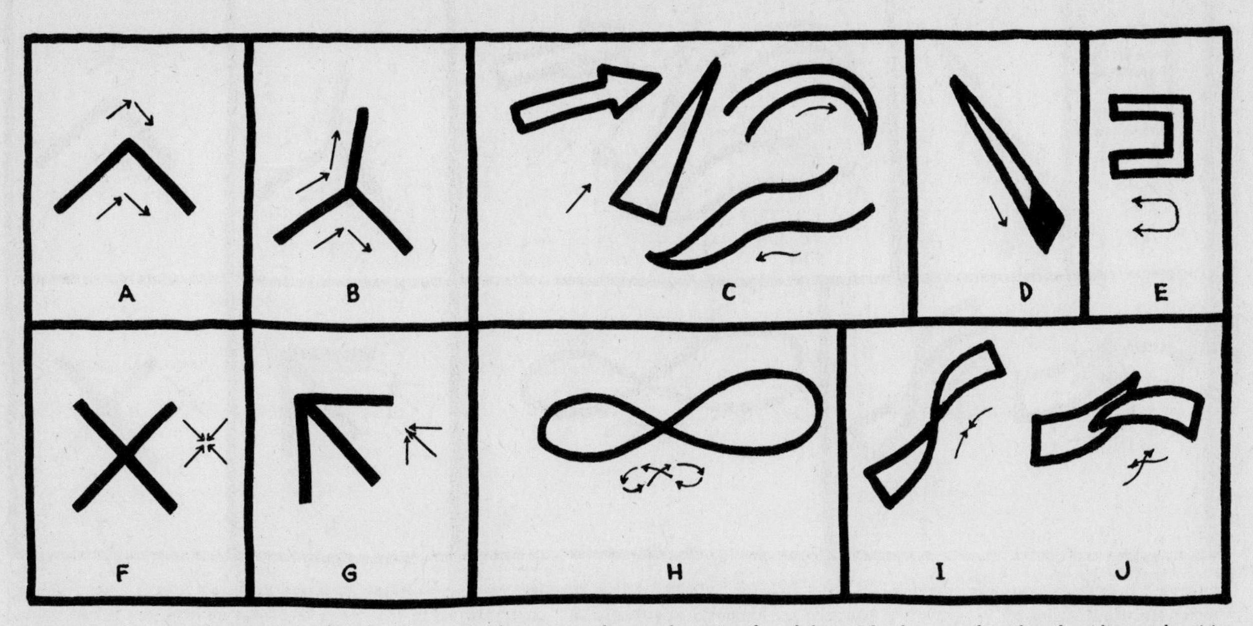

FIGURE 39. Lineal movement and static points. A. Shows natural eye path moving from left to right (because of occidental reading and writing habits, and so on), both on outer and inner sides of angular line. B. Another transitional line is added at the apex of the angle, illustrating how the eye will follow a path of least resistance. On the upper side the movement turns upward in the more rhythmic direction. On the under side the movement tends to follow the more angular line, being blocked by the angle at the right. C. Shows that the eye moves in the direction of the narrow end of a pattern, suggesting the pointing of an arrow. D. Illustrates how this rule may be broken by the addition of weight such as tone or color. E. Lines tied together in a right angle tend to begin movement at the middle and move outward toward both loose ends. F. Illustrates how a static point is created by lines crossing each other. G. Diagrams a static point made by a line converging at the corner of an angle. H. Shows that a cross-line static point may be partially overcome when the movement continues strongly after crossing. I. Diagram of two pointed patterns creating a static point by touching tip-to-tip. J. The static point is broken by overlapping the ends, letting the movement flow rhythmically from one to the other.

from form to form, from space to space, and throughout the picture as a whole.

Relationships of colors, tones, spaces, and lines are controlled and vitalized in the depth dimension by using the same unifying principles as before, developing thrusts and counterthrusts by means of receding or advancing planes.

THIRD-DIMENSIONAL LINE

Because of its transitional potentialities, line is a powerful agent in ordering cohesive sequences between forms and spaces from front to back and side to side in the prescribed picture field. Structural lines, either hidden or real, sew together forms and groups of forms on front, middle, and distance planes. They shape the separate parts and the whole into harmonious relationship within the limitations of the field in which they play. The eye of the observer can be led from unit to unit, from space to space, with linear point and counterpoint, to bring about visual beauties comparable to the aural beauties of a symphony.

Overlapping or lost and found lines establish direct recessional planes, especially when they are set at opposite directions (vertical against horizontal, and so on); that is, when some lines are lost or hidden behind others, they tend to set up recessive planes in relation to those in front. Many fine draftsmen use this line-overlapping idea to convey volume boundaries. It makes for looseness and play between the various planes on the volume contour and between the object and background, clarifying, yet at the same time unifying the several distance planes. It is a method to be used in works where line rather than space pattern is to dominate, because it tends to break the simple flatness of space contours and develop strong plastic recessions.

Combining light-dark contrast with overlapping line or pattern adds to the plastic effect, clearly drawing forms out from each other. The play between these overlapping planes may be dramatized by various light and dark accents along the contour edge if one is using line as the means (Figs. 50 and 51). In this way light and shade and strong form can be suggested by a drawing strictly in line.

Transitional lines create diagonal movements in and out or from side to side.

FIGURE 40. Control of three-dimensional movement. A. Diagram of a forceful third-dimensional recession, developed by overlapping planes in diminishing sizes. Arrows 2 and 3 show that negative spaces in sky and ground also create movement toward the point of perspective (4), making a static point at this place. B. Illustrates how strong recessions can be controlled by blocking the movement and turning it back toward the picture plane. Here the recession follows the tier of overlapping planes beginning at 1, is turned by plane 2, and returns along tier of overlapping planes (3). Group of planes 4 is added to turn the movement back into the picture again, creating a closed form. C. Illustrates the use of inverted perspective in controlling three-dimensional space. The movement from 1 to 4 tends to stay on a two-dimensional plane because, though the planes are overlapped as in A, the farthest ones are enlarged rather than diminished in size.

Upright and horizontal lines usually stay on the two-dimensional picture plane unless modified by other plastic means.

Delineation and coordination of planes are important. When two or more lines cross or touch each other (without defining planes by overlapping or other ways), a static point is created which in most cases is harmful to the form because it obstructs the harmonious flow and movement through various parts of the design. It also is harmful when lines or spaces tangle with edges of the frame or converge at corners or other obvious points. The same may be said in the case of colors that are different in some aspect, such as light-dark, but which because of other countermeans actually hold the same plane; and this is also true of tones and patterns. Focal points in the three-dimensional field can be established by lineal tensions and rhythms, developing an area or areas of dominance about which subjugated units and spaces revolve.

Lineal perspective, or convergence of lines at a distant point, is useful as a recessive means but must be considered as a plastic element in relation to the other three-dimensional quantities rather than merely as an illusory means of naturalism. Scientific perspective often needs to be completely reversed, or at least held in check, because of the necessity of holding the back plane in static relation to the picture plane, and of making a wall to stop and deflect the movement into a return transition toward the front of the field. The cold photographic likeness of forms is enhanced and given life and action by purposeful alteration of perspective line or space.

Lineal radiations from a point or tangential junctions on a line are principles of nature that may be used to advantage in creating a dominant feature.

THIRD-DIMENSIONAL SPACE

Positive space patterns or planes are made to take more distant positions by diminishing their size in relation to others near the front plane and by neutralizing the details of their contours. This coincides with the usual law of perspective in which nearest objects show the clearest and strongest contrasts (in tone, color, texture, and the rest) and objects become more neutral as they recede.

Another important way of developing a third dimension is by overlapping patterns, some of them being partly hidden behind others.

By using these two resources in conjunction, patterns, planes, and volumes may be recessed, advanced, and controlled at will to create transitions, contrasts, and focal points in the three-dimensional field. By knowing how to control planes in this way, one can recess the whole form into deep space, or by reversing the rule hold it to a flat, shallow range, depending on the particular want or need.

THIRD-DIMENSIONAL TONE

Juxtaposition of complementary tones is an important way of distinguishing plane edges, drawing out interior and exterior planes, manipulating them directionally, and defining their position in space.

In complete isolation from the other means, dark tones seem to recede and light tones advance, but the rule is so easily broken that it can hardly be called a rule. Such means as overlapping edges, diminishing line, color, tone, or space, easily overcome the rule. Many times the mere fact of association concerning subject matter will set tones, objects, or other things on certain planes, the illusion changing from one distance or directional plane to another at intervals in accordance with the way the mind's eye chooses to see it (Fig. 43). This mental-illusion factor is more significant in plane arrangement than is usually recognized.

Directional planes are disposed, as far as tone is concerned, largely by source illumination, that is, planes seem to take on certain facial directions (disregarding lineal perspective or other factors) because

*FIGURE 43. **Paranoid** Face, by Salvador Dali. An illustration of how tones in a picture will change recessive positions according to the imagined illusion at a given moment. View picture sideways to see image of woman's head. (Courtesy, Edward James. Photograph, Museum of Modern Art.)*

of relative degrees of light falling on them from some main source. The main light source, for example, coming from overhead and somewhat to the left will illuminate an object such as a cube so that top plane is lightest, left side medium, and right side darkest in tone.

In many instances in art structure there is need for compromise with certain opposing factors. An instance of this is the decorative use of tone values as against the use of the chiaroscuro, or light and shade, idea. If an artist were to go the whole way in developing planes by light and shade as suggested in the foregoing paragraph, he would do so at the expense of tonal design, or vice versa. Therefore, one should consider which is more important to the intended expression and compromise accordingly.

A practical method is to begin with one approach, such as that of tone-value design, and after this is set, to develop modeling within this, holding to the main tones in general but with enough variations within each tone to attain the desired form.

In nature, nearer things are seen to be in greater contrast and clarity, while farther things are more neutral in tone. When a neutral gray is seen with either black or white it most generally will take a more distant position. Taking advantage of this fact, planes can be advanced or recessed in three-dimensional space by areal perspective of tone.

In former times, when academic copying and imitation were the rule, the term "good drawing" had a meaning different from its present one. It meant exact transference of proportions and transitory effects

FIGURE 41. The Dream Ride, by William Glackens. General pictorial movement, lyrical and joyous, helps express the theme, dream ride. (Courtesy, New York Graphic Society.)

FIGURE 42. Analysis of Figure 41. Diagram of overlapping planes. Also an illustration of flattened, two-dimensional form.

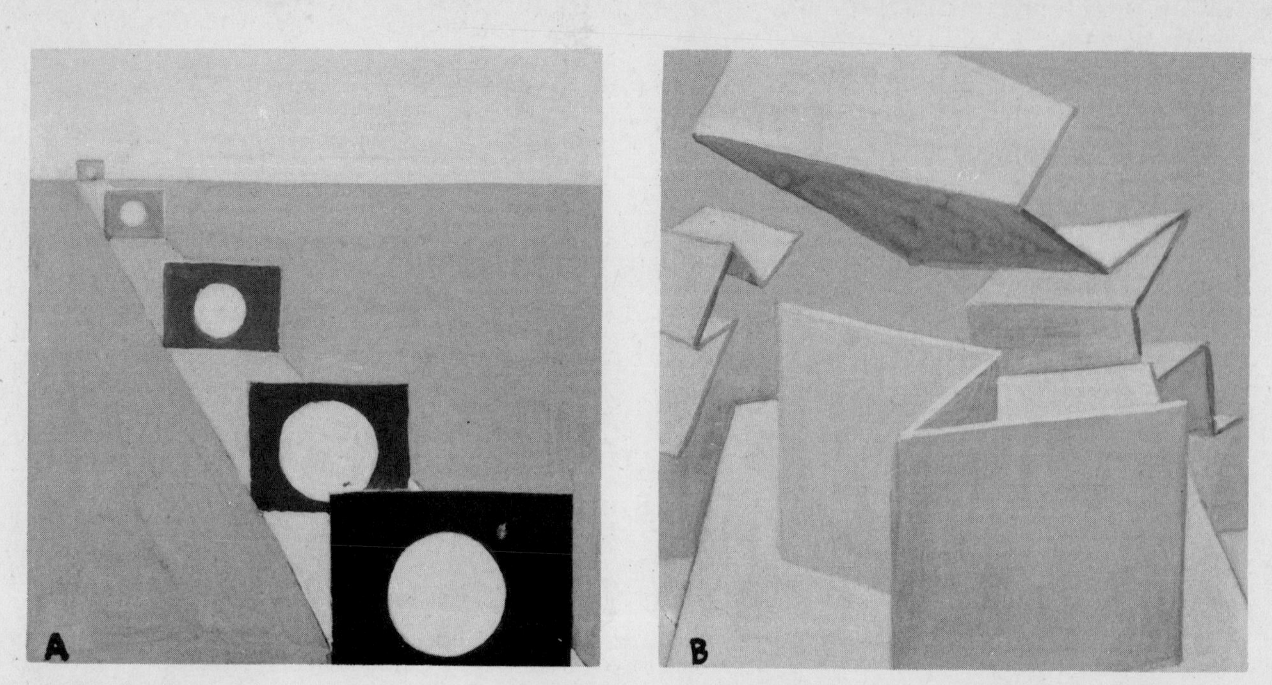

FIGURE 44. Tonal Planes. A. Diagram of distance planes, illustrating how both dark and light tones seem to recede when modified toward a neutral tone. B. Light-dark directional planes. An illustration of the way planes vary in tone value according to their facial direction in relation to the source of light.

of light and shadow from the model to the canvas. Today, "good drawing" means to draw forms or objects out from one another, to clearly coordinate and distinguish forms and planes. In the latter, the artist is the creator and master of his means. He goes directly to the core of the problem, eliminating superfluous lines, forms, and shadows that camouflage the thing he is trying to say.

Drawing out forms is accomplished largely by means of contrast and overlapping of plane edges; dark against light, color against complement, horizontal against vertical, and the rest. Opposites repel and separate forms from each other; analogies attract and bind.

Knowing such basic laws as these, the artist is able to work directly for plastic form. When using color, he applies each brush stroke as a plane, considering its value in relation to other planes, both distance and directional. The application is the same with tone values. When depicting a form such as a human figure, he is aware of the fact that when he changes tones he is making a new plane, and if he wants the form of a leg, for instance, to go around from front to side he merely makes another directional plane by making a tone or color that seems to recede in correct relation to the others. He dramatizes the complementary nature of the edges of these planes where they touch each other, clarifying and distinguishing each plane. In this way he pushes in and pulls out forms just as directly as though he were modeling with clay.

As we have said, opposites repel and analogies attract. By using the two in conjunction one can delineate planes and yet bind them into a whole that is strong and varied. The principle of contrast may be used in rhythmic sequence around single-form and group-form contours. This may be called *rhythmic contour*. It works with all the means—color, space, tone, and line. It is the lost and found play between the parts of a form, or one form and another.

Studying the cue in nature, we see that the exterior of a form such as a human body or limb is rhythmical in contour. Whereas on one side there will be a positive or convex hill, on the other there will be a negative or concave hollow. While these are opposites, there is a rhythmic play between the two when one follows along the form as a whole. One can accent these rhythms by playing thin lines against heavy ones, positive pattern contour against negative, dark against light, hard against soft, hue against complementary hue, brilliant against gray.

In all the means the negative accents usually will be placed at the points where the forms are most clearly separated from each other. Taking the human body as an example again, the heavier accents of line or tone, say, would come at the places where the forms

FIGURE 45. I'm Tired, by Yasuo Kuniyoshi. An example of this artist's sensitive drawing and design. (Collection, Whitney Museum of American Art.)

FIGURE 46. Analysis of Figure 45. Cubic solidity gained by control of light and shade. Plane directions accentuated by juxtaposing light against dark on interior of forms.

FIGURE 47. Analysis of Figure 45. Tones and textures used to direct movements through the design.

FIGURE 46.

FIGURE 47.

FIGURE 48. Bridge III, by Lyonel Feininger. This painting illustrates in an abstract way the principle of light-dark tone juxtaposition. (Courtesy, the artist.)

are most loosely connected with each other, such as at the bone and muscle joints or behind the ear or under the chin. When an artist uses this law with feeling, plus simplification and coordination of all the segments, he may be called a sensitive draftsman. This rule of accenting around a particular form is superseded many times by the rule of balancing accents over the design as a whole (Figs. 134 and 135).

THIRD-DIMENSIONAL COLOR

Distance color planes are forcefully separated by complementary juxtaposition of hue and intensity (cool color against warm, neutral against more intense). Generally speaking, warm colors like yellow-green, yellow, orange, and vermilion seem to take an advanced position while cool colors, like purple, violet, blue, and blue-green seem to recede. On the intensity side, relatively intense colors advance while neutralized (gray) ones recede.

Color analogies are instrumental in creating planes on single volumes or objects. The rule might be stated like this: "The shadow color of an object always goes toward the complementary of the highlight." It may be added that this also works with tone value and intensity. The hue on the lighted side of an object is usually more warm and intense and the shaded side more cool and gray, but often the reverse is true, as of objects in strong sunlight. The degree to which a shadow color will be found around the color circle toward the highlight's complement also depends on the amount of light thrown on the object. The more light, the farther around toward its complement the shadow will go. The master uses these and other laws subtly and sparingly.

The mistake most novices make in using color is in attempting to create various color planes by merely changing the light-dark value (usually by adding white) but failing to change the hue or intensity. This results in a chalky appearance and does little to create different planes. If the planes are right, the color will be right.

Analogous color harmonies and rhythms create movement and transition, connecting units and groups of units in the three-dimensional field, giving life and completeness to the form as a whole.

Color is a strong means of deciding or modifying the focal point in three-dimensional organization, defining a central figure around which volumes, planes, and movements function and revolve.

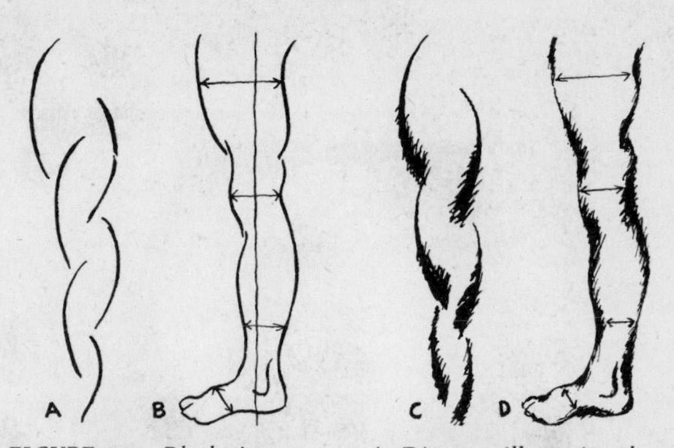

FIGURE 50. Rhythmic contour. A. Diagram illustrating the abstract basis of rhythmic pattern contour. B. Anatomical detail, showing how the principle works in nature, the arrows indicating convex curves on one side opposed by concave ones on the other. C. Diagram illustrating the abstract basis of rhythmic tone or accented line. D. Anatomical detail, showing how this principle works in nature.

FIGURE 49. The Blacksmith, by Ivan L. Albright. A complexity of coordinated details, delineated by light-dark juxtaposition. (Courtesy, Art Institute of Chicago.)

FIGURE 51. Merry Gatherings in the Magic Jar (detail), by Kung Kai, A. D. 960-1280. An example of accented line. (Collection, Metropolitan Museum of Art.)

THIRD-DIMENSIONAL TEXTURE

Texture has plastic values as well as decorative, although these are largely useful to development of distance planes rather than directional.

Loud textures (those made up of strong contrasts of tone, color, or pattern) advance; quiet ones recede. In this way either volumes or negative areas, according to structural need, may be modified to function plastically in advancing or receding positions.

Besides the foregoing plastic uses of texture, it is important as a means of symbolizing realistic values, such as the hardness of rocks, softness of clouds, roughness of tree bark, smoothness of metal, and so on. This might be called its expressive value. Its other use is a decorative one. Matisse, Rousseau,

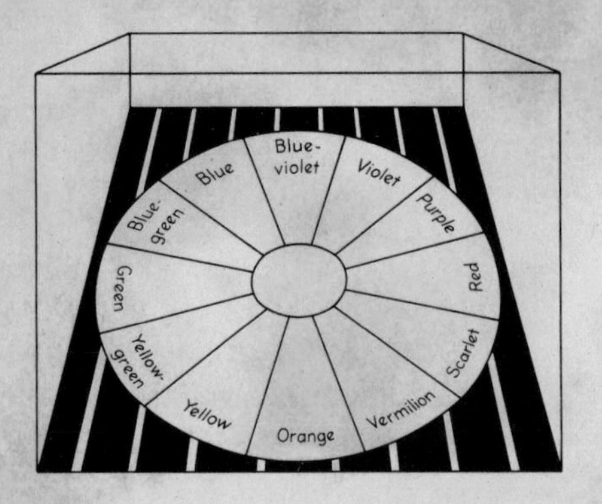

FIGURE 52. Color-receding diagram, showing which hues in their natural intensities seem to take relatively near or far positions is space.

Van Gogh, Kuniyoshi, and others, in their individual ways, use texture as an added decorative refinement. Using textures as a decorative means is tantamount to eliminating a strong third-dimensional recession; for when pattern textures are repeated and spread decoratively over the whole picture area, the flat two-dimensional plane is emphasized.

All the other aesthetic tools, line, color, space, and tone, besides the plastic values, of course, have expressive and decorative ones, the latter having been suggested in outlining the means in relation to the two-dimensional plane.

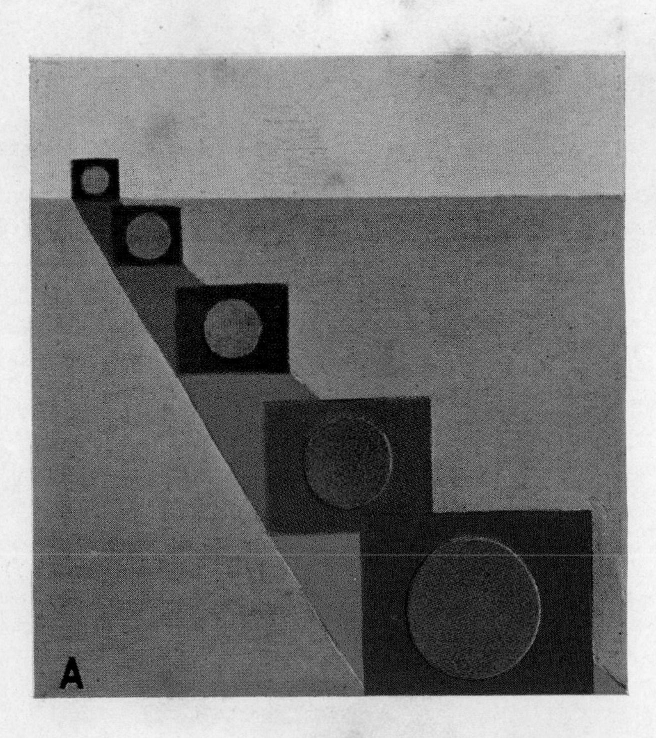

FIGURE 53. A. Diagram of color distance planes, showing how colors seem to recede when the intensity is modified toward gray. Note also that colors change in tone value as they recede. B. Diagram of color directional planes, illustrating that, as each plane receives more or less light, it also changes in color in a natural transition around the color wheel. The addition of intensity modification as in A would add to the plastic form.

7. VOLUMES, PLANES AND THE TOTAL MEANS

When an artist creates a consistent entity—a new organic structure within the canvas—he becomes a small god, so to speak, organizing a new world out of the elements, uniting them by the same principles of nature that give life and stability to the universe.

For realization of volumes, movement, and the total means the picture builder may again be mindful of the universal examples of space-volume unity and vitality—the solar and atomic systems where are found dominant central nuclei around which subdominant forms revolve. The particular forms in rhythmic animation, changing, balancing, and adjusting, all work in relation to each other and to the entire system. Motion and movement are initiated by positive-negative forces in counteraction—unified systems existing for a time through this process of reconciliation of opposites. Eventually, the elements separate, disintegrate, and return to chaotic formlessness, later again to be enveloped and to take part in construction of another system, animated, equalized, and complete. The universe, and all its elements, is given continued and everlasting form and life by this construction-destruction process: some units for a time attract and hold others in check, creating a mass or system which in itself revolves around a more dominant system, and so on from atoms to infinite universes.

Two most important principles to be learned by the artist-creator from this universal example are vitality and unity. In unity there is balance, completeness, and perfection. In vitality there is force, movement, energy, and life.

As we have shown in the foregoing chapters, each of the plastic means in isolation has certain advancing-receding properties which are valuable in three-dimensional design. But in the interest of a higher law we must remember that seldom in a good work of painting or sculpture are any of the means found in isolation, but many and sometimes all of them are interwoven and combined to create volumes, tensions, rhythms, and total form. And each singly detached rule is either modified or foiled by more dominant use of one or more of the other laws. The artist's problem is to organize all the structural elements within and in relation to the prescribed field, balancing weight against weight, force against force, movement against movement, creating an organism that in its sum total is alive and complete.

An understanding of this principle of pictorial dynamics is the end to be attained in design education and cannot be stressed too much or too often. Consideration of the artist's means and the relationship of these to the principles of unity in the previous chapters was merely preliminary to this end. By first studying the ways and means intellectually, the student may gain a knowledge that will later help him to attain dynamically unified creations through intuitive means.

The emotions and feelings controlled and ordered by taste and reason must necessarily predominate in this creative process. Every line, color, tone, and brush stroke must have significance and relationship to every other element, and to the theme, technique, and design as a whole. As each stroke is added, the artist must feelingly and instinctively relate it to all past strokes and every stroke yet to come. A picture is finished when the theme is expressed in total completeness, when not a stroke or tittle could be added or subtracted without unbalancing the whole.

The artist must consider the eventual spectator and design the elements so that his vision will be led onto the pictorial stage and directed through main visual paths and secondary areas, finally coming to rest on a focal point usually located near the center of the field.

Because the bottom edge of the canvas is the closest perspective point, the eye path usually begins somewhere to one side on this plane; then moves upward and inward, skirting one of the side walls of the field until it reaches the backdrop limits; edges along these from one side to the other until stopped by the other side wall; is thrust into a reverse movement back toward the frontal plane; and spirals into the focal point, usually coming to rest there with minor move-

FIGURE 54. Le Guéridon, by Georges Braque. A painting with emphasis placed on pattern and texture variation. (Courtesy, Paul Rosenberg Gallery.)

ments continuing on out to the frontal base. The ways in which eye movement may begin, move, or end are limitless and should not and cannot be outlined by rule; can one only say that the rough outline just given generally holds true. At least, it is a pattern that may be followed as a first introduction to the problem, later to be scrapped for a more intuitive plan. This also goes for the other instances where we have illustrated this eye movement idea by the use of arrows. The point is not that our charting of the movement in such cases is the only way the eye may follow through the picture, but that one should develop some such way of "reading" a composition so as to understand the "story" of the picture.

In picture building there are two distinct types of "planes." We differentiate between the two by calling one *distance plane* and the other *directional plane*. The first refers to a certain place, area, or position, in measured relation to the front, back, or sides, of the picture-field boundaries (Fig. 61*A*). Picture plane, foreground plane, middle plane, background plane are all examples of distance planes. The second refers to the facial direction of planes like upright, oblique, horizontal, and so on (Fig. 61*B*). Examples are sky plane, ground plane, side plane, cubic plane, surface plane, and parallel plane.

As already suggested in the foregoing chapter, considered apart from other formal means, distance planes are established mainly by means of perspective or diminishing size. Other things being equal, large volumes or planes take a near position while small

FIGURE 55. Central Park, by George Grosz. Water colors set on paper with an emotional, childlike freedom, with sensitiveness to textural and lineal values. (Courtesy, Associated American Artists, Inc.)

ones seem to recede. Other means, like overlapping edges, advancing color or tone, or transferred nature values, serve to overcome or modify the rule.

If one is to have real control over the problem of light and shade, the attention must be focused on directional planes, the basic element in the study. By learning to manipulate and arrange these planes in a direct manner by changing the amount of light-dark on each, one is able not only to control the general source of light but also to organize the planes in directional sequences and balances to attain vitality and design. This is another instance of the creative attitude's being superior to the imitative. The academic method depends on the superficial and momentary effects of light and shade, having no real control over significant form or net unity.

Besides the light-dark values in turning planes in various facial directions, a relative change of hue and color intensity is needed. In forming these different plane faces, rhythms and analogies are largely used, running toward contrasts at the plane edges to accentuate and define each plane and its relative facial direction. As an example, if an octagonal form were the object to be painted, each directional plane would have an analogous relation to the planes next to it, not only in tone value but also in hue and intensity.

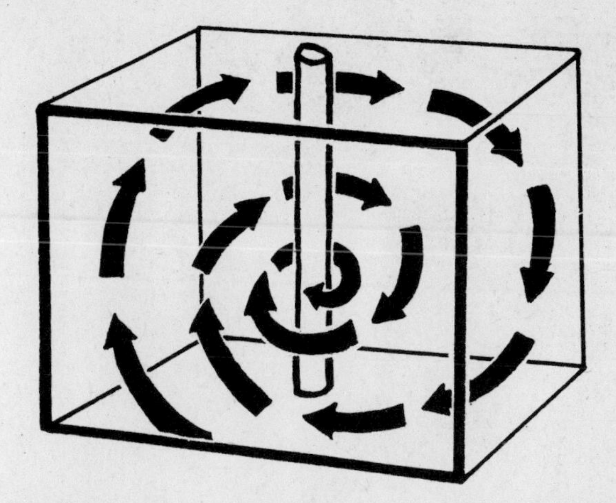

FIGURE 57. Diagram of average three-dimensional movement within the picture field.

FIGURE 56. Analysis of Figure 55. Vitality and animation, depicted with dynamic space patterns, the whole unified by repeating and rhyming characteristic shapes.

Forms are delineated and clarified when tone and color contrasts on plane edges are exaggerated. On the more or less flat bas-relief type of form the complementary tone and color juxtaposition is stressed at the contour edge. On the cubic or full type of form the contrast is emphasized on the interior edges of the planes that make up each volume. For unity's sake either the interior or exterior is given emphasis, but rarely both.

Direct modeling of planes and volumes is essential, at least in early studies. All cast shadows and other superficial things which tend to camouflage the basic form should be eliminated for reasons of clarification. Later on, shadows may be used for decorative, expressive, or other reasons if they serve a real purpose.

Overlapping of space-contour edges is a means of developing distance planes, and unless combined with lineal perspective, such planes remain directionally parallel to the two-dimensional surface. Nearest planes naturally catch the eye first, and the patterns covered most by overlapping take a more distant place. In this way planes can be arranged to suit the needs of plastic inward-outward movement and repose.

Grouping of distance planes is important to clearly define each plane and avoid confusion of movement and form. In other words, enough dominant volumes or plane surfaces should exist on each given distance position (like picture plane, middle plane, or backdrop plane) to establish clearly the existence of an allover plane at that place. Other planes of subordinate character can be part of the distance plane

FIGURE 58. FIGURE 59.

FIGURES 58 and 59. Still Life with Purple Flowers, by Henry Rasmusen, 1943. Painting by the author and an analysis, showing eye path charted around and into center of interest, ending in upward sweep fanning out at the top. Here the movement is developed primarily by directional plane relationships, the various planes of table, flowerpot, floor, and so on, being twisted and adjusted with each other in rhythms of facial direction and contour line. (Collection, Utah State Institute of Fine Arts.)

masses or be scattered through the negative areas between.

The farthest or background plane should be simplified even more than others as a limit or foil against which the total action takes place; usually it is seen to be parallel to the front or picture plane. This back plane may be likened to the backdrop curtain on a theater stage. The picture plane, likened to a transparent front curtain, may be defined as being on a line perpendicular to the bottom edge of the picture.

Because things with natural gravity are based on or grow out of a horizontal ground plane, a picture is usually more stable and right when this foundation weight is suggested, and upward movement from the close foreground is accentuated. The only way a picture seems stable otherwise is when weights are equalized over the whole surface. In general, even the shapes of particular objects or forms in a picture give more of a feeling of stability if their shapes suggest heavier bases, such as the horizontal base line and arched tops of hills, shrubbery, or human figures.

Directional as well as distance planes are unified and given spirit and action in relation to each other by bringing into play the law of rhythm, repetition, opposition, and variation. Distance planes are repeated at varied intervals from front to back, from side to side, and are placed in certain controlled positions throughout the picture field, so the eye is led from place to place, from space to form to space with rhythmic timing, movement, and poise.

Upright planes are played against horizontal, right oblique against left oblique, and movement is created and controlled by rhythmic chords of plane direction, size, and position. Plane is played against plane, volume against volume, space against form against space. Directional faces are played together in rhythms and counterpoint, like forms repeated with variation—forms of opposite characteristics, directions, or positions played in contrast.

Positive volumes (the solid forms made up of planes, colors, tones, and other means) and their relation to negative space constitute the most impor-

FIGURE 60. Landscape, by Theodore Robinson. A picture illustrating uncontrolled movement, the eye being forced to follow the violently moving path in and out of the field in one swoop (compare with Figures 1 and 92). (Collection, Whitney Museum of American Art.)

tant element or at least the most basic consideration in plastic design. Volumes must be in correct relation one to another and to the surrounding negative spaces to ensure movement, poise, and unity.

Where planes combine to make solid volumes, the contour shape of each plane and the pattern of the whole solid, as well as the air or background shapes left around it, must continue to be considered for interest and variety of contour.

Relatively speaking, volumes are given more bulk and strength by being built of positive convex planes in the whole structure and leaving less area for the

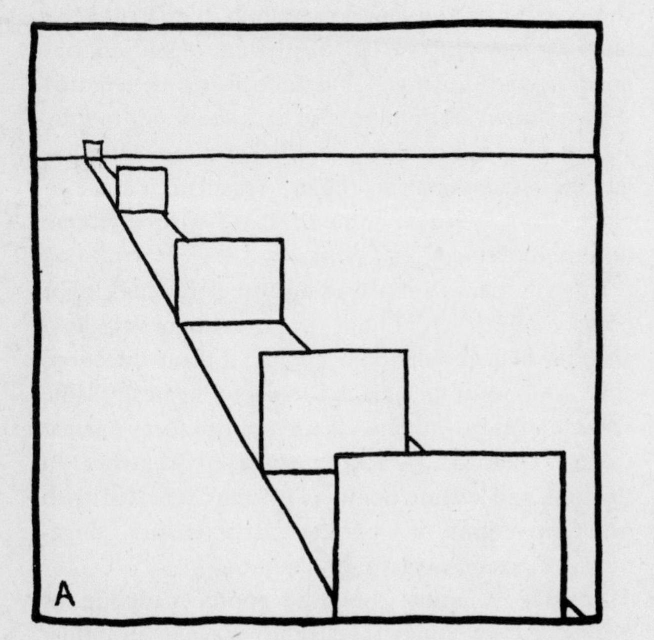

FIGURE 61. A. Diagram of space distance planes, showing how space patterns seem to recede when reduced in size. B. Diagram of directional planes, showing space patterns facing in various directions.

FIGURE 62. The Return of the Herd, by Pieter Brueghel.

FIGURE 63. Analysis of Figure 62. Three-dimensional wedge-shaped volumes moving in and out of the picture field, giving spatial reality to the form.

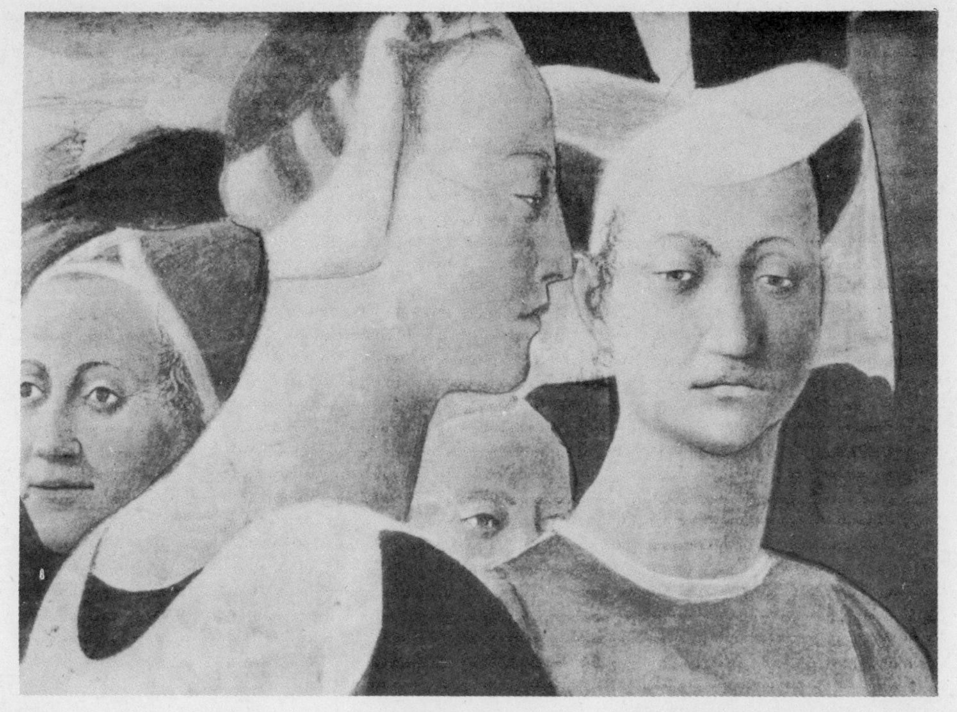

FIGURE 64. Retinue of Queen Saba (detail), by Piero Della Francesca. An example of two-dimensional type of form.

concave portions. This works for single volumes as well as for the whole design. Simplicity of volumes is important but not necessarily better than complexity if (an important if) the intricacies are in subordinate relation to the larger mass in which they exist.

Expression of any idea (objective or nonobjective) is made more immediately powerful when all the elements are designed with the principle of mass dominance kept in mind. For instance, the color unity and effectiveness are strengthened when one general color dominates the whole picture leaving the complementary in a subordinate role. Within the major color area can be played minor sequences and secondary rhythms, related but subordinate to the larger mass. The same is true with tone, for example, a dominant over-all tone (usually medium) with focal

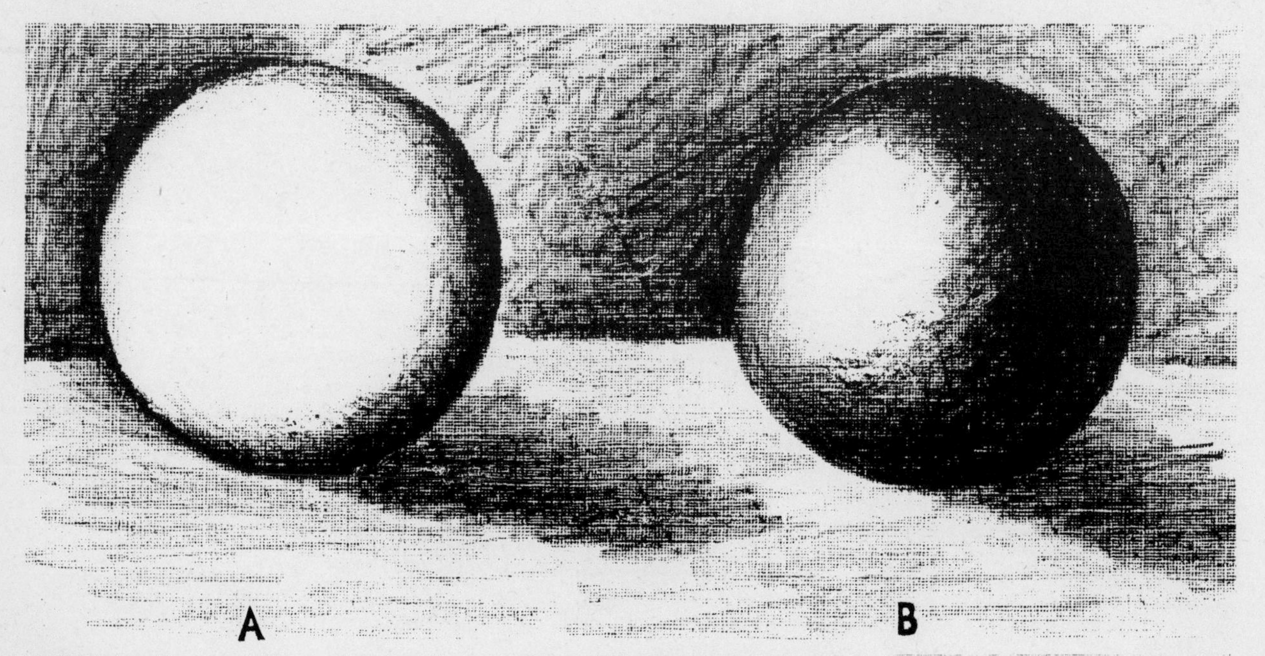

FIGURE 65. Two types of form. A. Sphere illustrating flattened two-dimensional effect achieved by accentuating the outer contour. B. Sphere in full-rounded form achieved by accentuating light-dark contrasts on the interior planes.

FIGURE 66. Mental Calculus, by René Magritte. An example of full three-dimensional forms in deep space. (Collection, Mrs. Stanley Resor. Photograph, courtesy, Museum of Modern Art.)

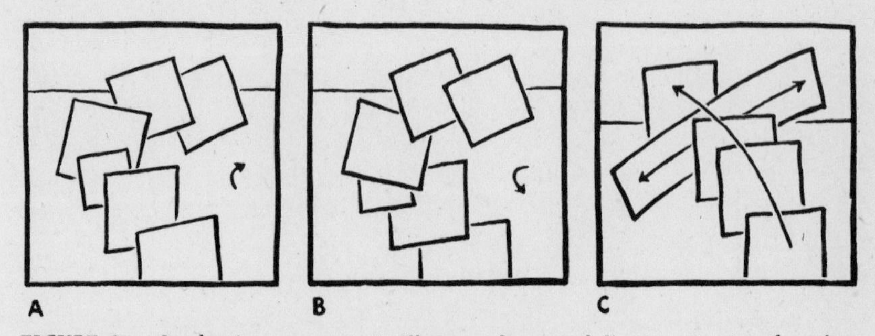

FIGURE 67. Overlapping patterns. A. Illustrates the natural direction of action, from front to back. B. Indicates how movement can be reversed by changing the order of overlapping. C. Illustrates a combination of two- and three-dimensional movement. The overlapping planes, beginning at the picture plane and receding toward the back, direct movement into the three-dimensional field. The long pattern crossing through these planes develops a two-dimensional movement parallel to the picture plane.

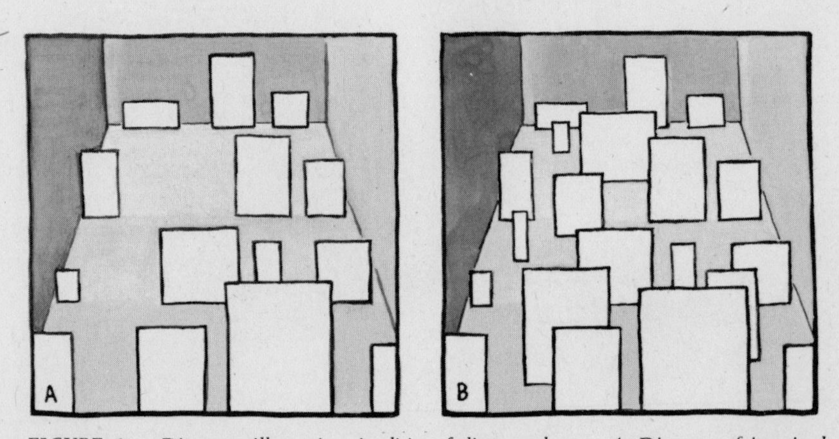

FIGURE 68. Diagrams illustrating simplicity of distance planes. A. Diagram of imagined pictorial stage with planes placed at five simple distance points. B. The same planes with others added between them, illustrating how this adds confusion and breaks the unity of the three-dimensional design and blocks the eye movement in and out of the pictorial field.

FIGURE 69. Card Players, by Paul Cézanne. (Courtesy, Barnes Foundation.)

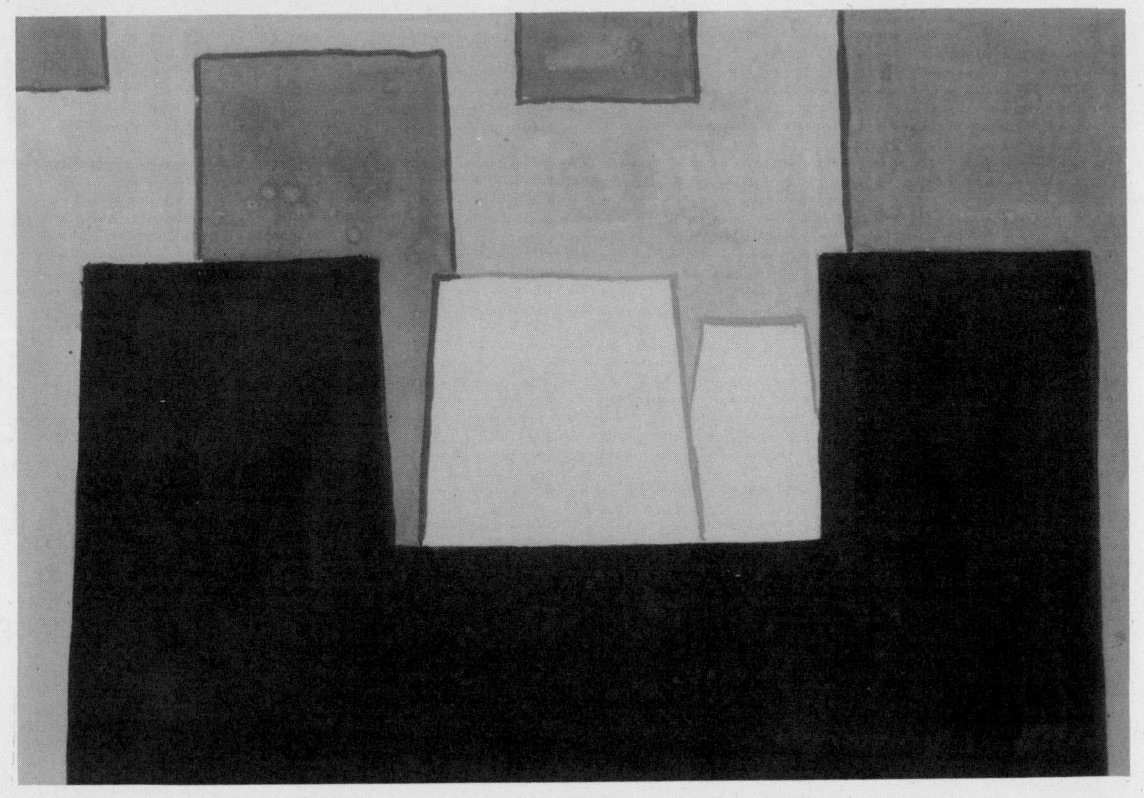

FIGURE 70. Analysis of simplified distance planes in Figure 69.

FIGURE 71. The City, by Peter Grippe. An illustration of three-dimensional directional planes. (Collection, Museum of Modern Art.)

point in contrasting light or dark. As to line, a picture is given strength when certain lineal directions dominate, like upright or horizontal lines carrying the main theme, with others of diagonal or other nature being seen less often in the design.

Dominant and subordinate directional planes should be arranged in the same way. Dark-light simplification on single planes and volumes clarifies and emphasizes their form. This is done by limiting the number of tones used in modeling the planes. From the standpoint of light and shade we may put it this way for initial experiments: Form may be simplified by limiting the lighting of single or many volumes to one main light source. Other sources of direct or reflected light should remain secondary and subordinate, if used.

In developing transition and balance through the picture, the general directional movement of volumes (the axis or center of weight) must be considered as well as the lineal contour. The principles of balance, transition, variation, and domination are all important in unifying and ordering space and volume on the pictorial stage. Receding movements and transitions on one side are balanced by advancing movements on the other side. Weighty volumes are played against lighter ones, contrapuntal movements added to enrich main drives, axial directions rhymed or repeated, and opposed.

Large volumes can be set back and modified by recessive coloring, small volumes given more importance or advanced to closer positions by more insistent texture, tone, color, or some other means. In this way all the means are fused into the total design.

Movement tensions—forces straining or stretching

against one another—are useful in developing balance between volumes and lending vitality to the work. These tensions are created by the usual means of advancing-receding planes and must be used for net unity, force pulling against force, giving vitality and equilibrium to directional and distance movements.

Tensions are best understood by first considering how they work within a single pattern and later relating this knowledge to solid volumes and the third dimension.

As pointed out in earlier chapters, movement is induced (where pattern is concerned) when certain shapes are pointed at one end or when the shape is longer in one dimension and shorter in the other (Fig. 39*C*). The stronger movement or force in each case is in the direction of the greater length. A lesser or subordinate movement or tension exists across the shorter width of the pattern, and where these two movements cross, there is a central point which we call the axial center. When the two dimensions are

FIGURE 72. Bust from the Ivory Coast, Africa. Keen adjustment of planes and volumes. (Collection, Barnes Foundation.)

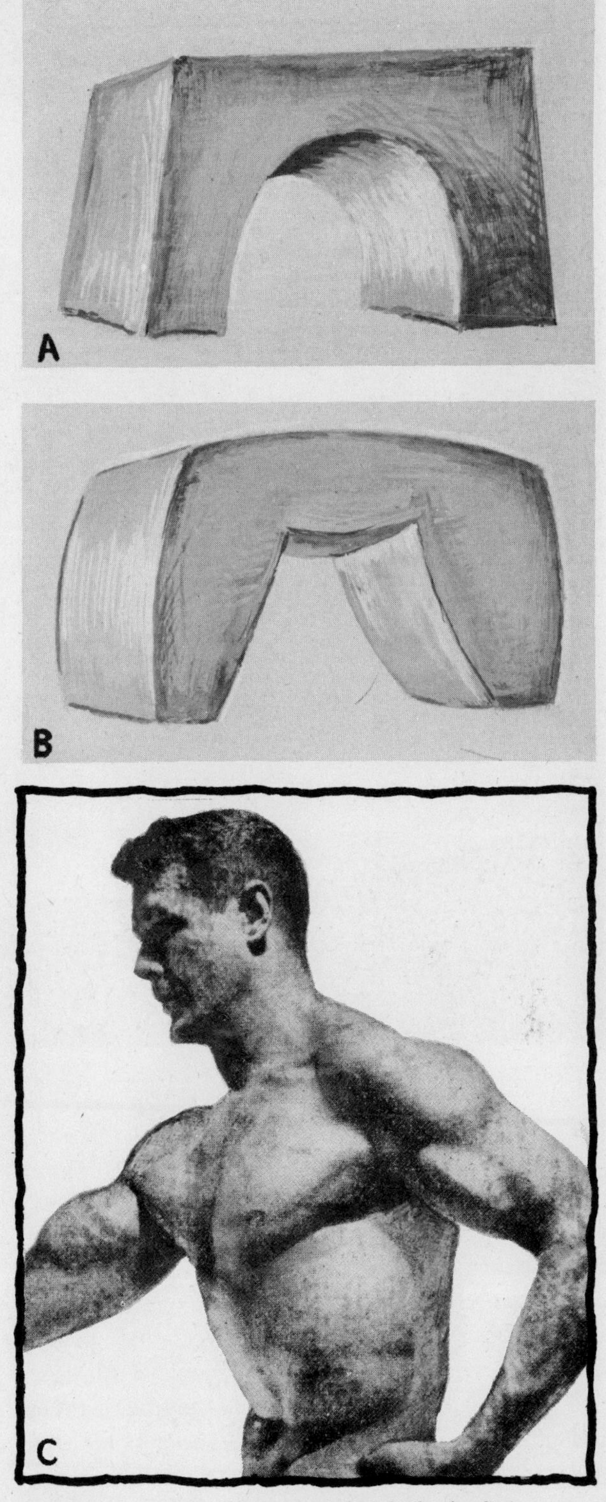

FIGURE 73. Positive form. A. A form built of ordinary contour planes. B. A form illustrating attainment of volume by building up positive planes. C. An example of positive form in nature.

FIGURE 74. Strength through simplicity. A. A cube, showing simplified directional planes, contrasting with the jumbled, incoherent mass in B.

FIGURE 75. Emerveillment, by José De Creeft. An example of positive form, sometimes referred to as volume. (Collection, Metropolitan Museum of Art.)

FIGURE 76. *FIGURE 77.*

FIGURES 76 and 77. Two Children, by William Zorach. The author's analysis indicates directional planes simplified into four main sides of the group. (Courtesy, Downtown Gallery.)

FIGURE 78. The Miracle of St. Ignatius de Loyola, by Rubens. One of this old master's most successful works.

FIGURE 79. Analysis of Figure 78. Twisting, overlapping volumes here lead the eye into and out of third-dimensional space.

equal, the pattern can be called a static shape because there is an equal strain across this central point. In a more complex shape, such as a cross, the movement or tension is still stronger along the greater length, just as in a simple long rectangle. A pattern is weakened when the contours are so complex as to become the dominant force, subordinating the larger shape.

Carrying the idea of tensions further, we find that the negative or background spaces contain the same dynamic or static movement according to the size or shape of the area in relation to the positive spaces. Where the tension is dynamic in the positive pattern, it will create a negative tension in the background (Fig. 81*A*).

Now relating this knowledge to the third dimension, starting with flat planes, we see that there exist certain tensions between axial centers of the various planes as well as the axial centers of the negative surrounding areas. In order to realize the existence of these tensions it is necessary to use the imagination to some extent, because the movement or tension exists from point to point in a spacial depth that is more imaginary than real.

As in a two-dimensional space, the stronger pull is in the direction of the longer axial line (imaginary or real) between planes or forms. The greater the relative space interval the greater the tension.

By tipping the axes in relation to each other, the tension is made greater where the forms are farthest apart and lesser where they are closer together, thus making a generally more active and dynamic relationship between the several planes (Fig. 82). This is one of the reasons for tipping or distorting natural shapes, to give them added life and vitality; in the same way greater tensions are created within single objects by distorting the character of the contour.

Tensions in relation to solid volumes is a more complex subject, but the same principles already considered hold true. The only difference is that solid volumes have more plane surfaces, and each of these has to be considered in relation to the other and the surrounding areas (Fig. 83*A*).

Not to be overlooked is the fact that tensions between volumes and negative spaces of the picture can be modified or nullified by such means as tensions between colors, tones, textures, and the other formal methods. These tensional movements exist between things of a like character; as when a color like vermilion is repeated or rhymed from one side of the picture to another, a tension is created between these two points. Opposite forces repel; harmonious ones attract.

Unity is broken and the picture field violated either when any volume or plane thrusts forward past the picture plane or when the back plane is vacant or filled with receding holes, and the vision is allowed to wander uncontrolled into distant space. As with all the other plastic means, there must be a right relationship between the volumes and frame of the field, all the enclosed design harmonizing with, and becoming part of, a total form that is consistently enclosed by the shell of the outer frame.

The picture plane (Fig. 35) is the most important in regard to total unity because it is the basic surface on which the form is built—the screen upon which all the action takes place. This plane is essentially two-dimensional, and although the total field may be recessed in a relative depth, the total form should still

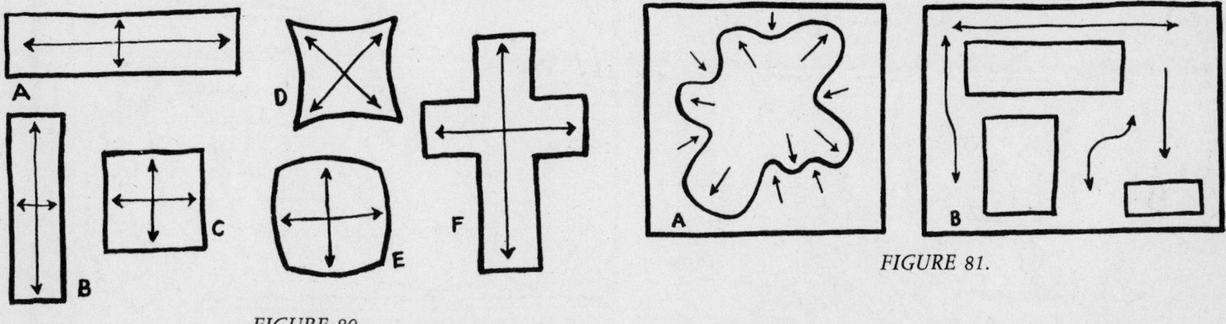

FIGURE 80.

FIGURE 81.

FIGURE 80. Two-dimensional tensions. A. A rectangular-shaped pattern in horizontal position, with the movement going toward each end, suggesting how relative movements create dynamic tensions within a flat shape, depending on its general character and placement. B. The same principle working in an upright direction. C. A shape equal in each dimension creates a static tension. D. A static shape in which the tension is diagonal because of the expansion at the corners. E. The tension is vitalized at the four sides by expanding the contour at these places. F. A complex shape composed of A and B, and the resulting dynamic tension, the longer direction having the stronger pull or tension.

FIGURE 81. Two-dimensional tensions in positive and negative space. A. A complex positive pattern, the arrows suggesting the tension moving outward toward the expanded contours. In the outer area one can see how tensions also exist in negative spaces, the movements pushing toward the inverted parts of a positive shape. B. Tensions exist in negative spaces, depending on the general character or shape. At the upper left corner is seen a static point created by two negative patterns of the same width, converging at a corner. At the upper right the movement turns the corner rhythmically because of the varied widths. The arrow at the right suggests how the tension can be greater in a negative area, depending on the relative sizes of the negative and positive spaces.

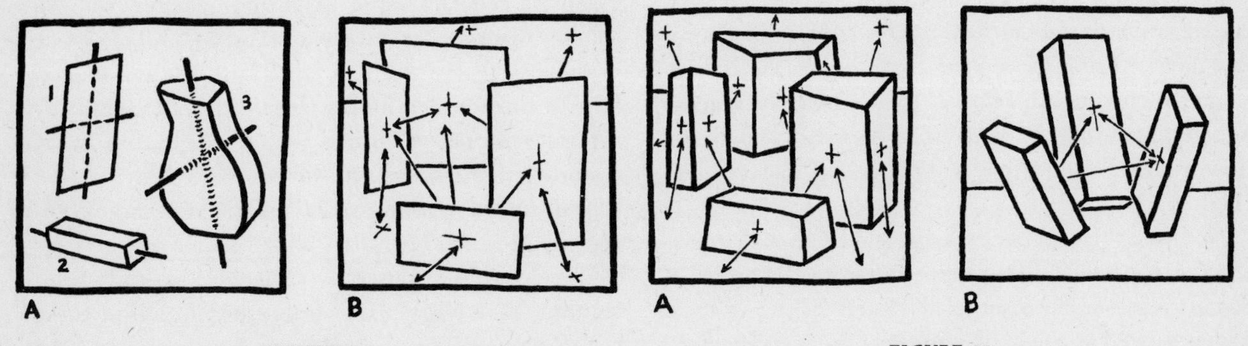

FIGURE 82.

FIGURE 83.

FIGURE 82. Axes, and tensions of plane and volume. A. Axis lines in various types of forms. 1 is a diagram of long and short axes in a flat object. 2 shows the main central axis in a cubed object. 3 illustrates the long and short axes of a complex, irregular form. B. The attraction or tension between planes, measured by the amount of space between the axes of the various forms and the dynamic or static relationships. (Adapted from Erle Loran, Cézanne's Composition.)

FIGURE 83. Tension between volumes. A. A group of solid volumes, the crosses and arrows indicating tensions between the various surface planes. B. The dynamic tension between volumes is increased by tipping the axes in relation to one another. (Adapted from Erle Loran, Cézanne's Composition.)

FIGURE 84. Industry-Iron, mural detail by Thomas Benton. An illustration of the flat wall plane destroyed by strong perspective. Also, figure at right is an example of a form thrusting forward past picture plane, violating the closed-field principle. (Courtesy, The New School for Social Research.)

retain a strong parallel relation to this two-dimensional plane.

A static plane in relation to the picture plane is one that stands parallel with it. A dynamic plane is one that stands diagonally in relation to the picture plane (Fig. 85).

Forms are brought into more harmonious relation to the picture plane by reversing or modifying ordinary scientific perspective of all the means (Fig. 86*C*), by using transparent planes (Fig. 86*A*), interwoven planes (Fig. 86*B*), or conjunctural lines (Fig. 86*D*). Lines, instead of converging in the distance, would be modified to run parallel to each other in a more vertical direction. Diagonal directional planes would be modified toward a more parallel relation to the picture plane. Patterns and volumes, instead of becoming smaller as they recede, would be made larger (Fig. 86*C*), the sense of third dimension being attained by overlapping edges (Fig. 40*C*).

Instead of colors being grayed or cooled at more distant places, they would be given the same, or nearly the same strengths as the nearer planes. Strong textures would be used on background objects to modify their recessive positions. Ground planes and sky planes are flattened and tipped into more vertical direction, in more static relation to the picture plane. In this way the form as a whole is compressed into a more limited and controlled depth, in more harmonious relation to the picture plane.

Recent nonrepresentational works show an experi-

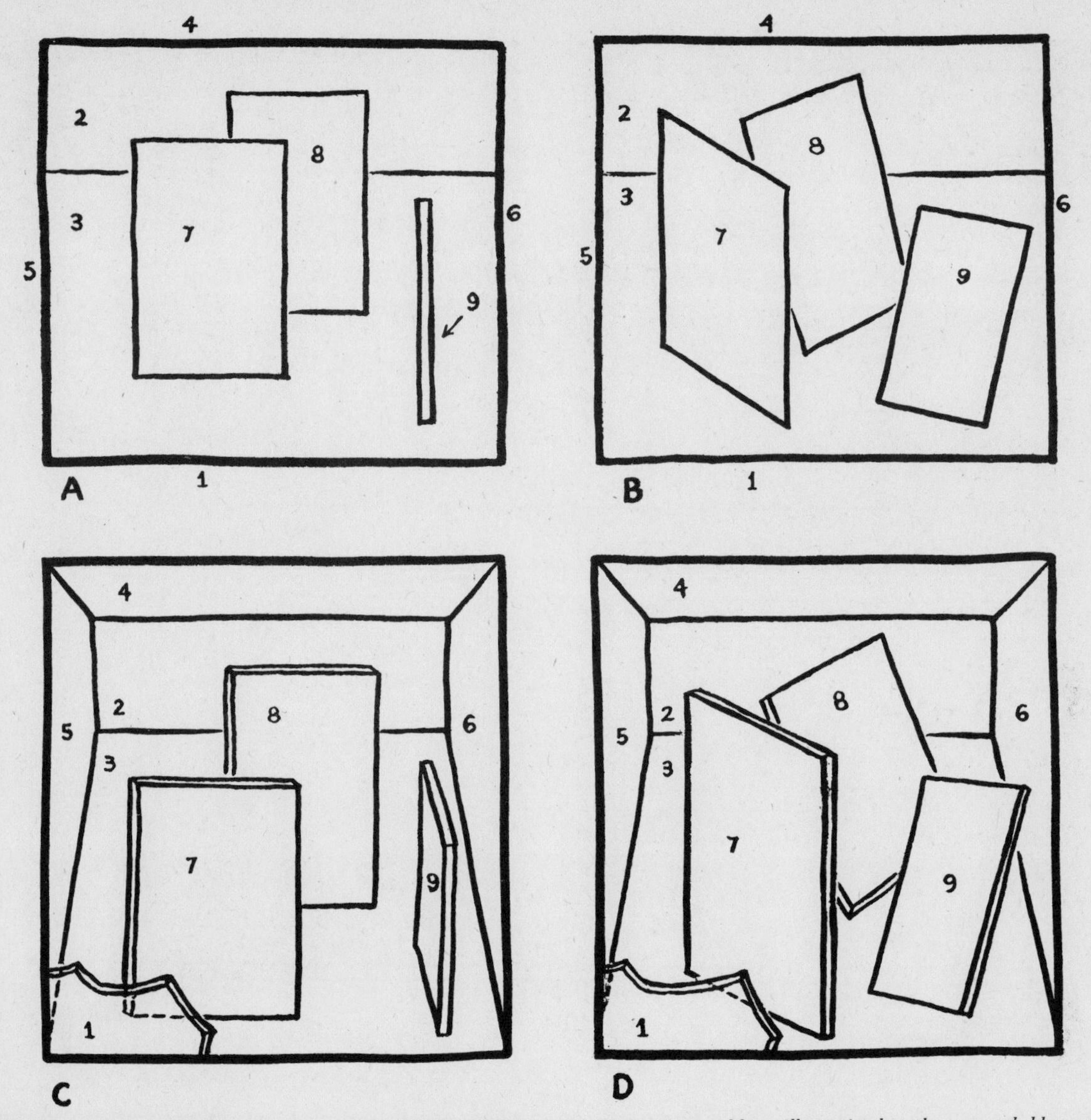

FIGURE 85. Static and dynamic planes. A. Group of planes made of horizontal and vertical lines, illustrating how they seem to hold to a parallel direction in relation to the picture plane and other dimensions of the field. These are called static or parallel planes. B. A group of diagonal planes in dynamic relation to the picture plane and the field, with the exception of upright edges of plane 7, which are in static relation to the sides of the field (5 and 6) and the picture plane 1. C. and D. Three-dimensional illustrations of A and B, showing more clearly the planes in relation to the picture plane (cross section 1), rear wall (2), ground plane (3), sky plane (4), and side wall planes (5 and 6). D. Shows more clearly the dynamic relation between the tipping and diagonal planes and the walls of the field. (Adapted from Erle Loran, Cézanne's Composition.)

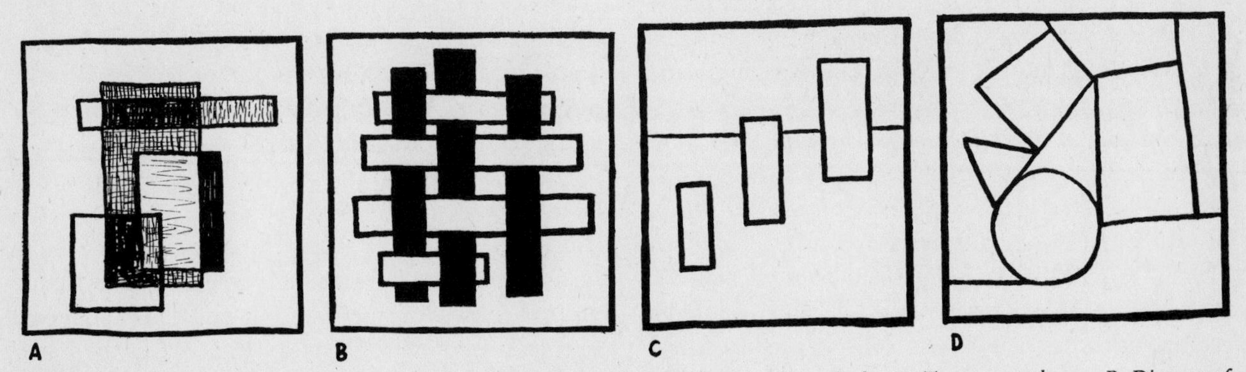

FIGURE 86. Diagrams illustrating ways in which a two-dimensional picture plane may be retained. A. Transparent planes. B. Diagram of interwoven planes. C. Reversed lineal perspective. D. Conjunctural lines.

FIGURE 87. My Egypt, by Charles Demuth. A painting illustrating the use of transparent planes. (Collection, Whitney Museum of Amer·ican Art.)

FIGURE 89. Les Saltimbanques, by Fernand Léger. An example of interwoven planes. (Courtesy, Jacques Seligmann Galleries.)

FIGURE 88. Victime des Indépendants, by Amédée Ozenfant. Two-dimensional surface retained by use of conjunctural lines. (Courtesy, Passedoit Gallery.)

FIGURE 90. Table Tops, by Henri Burkhard. An example of reversed perspective. (Collection, Whitney Museum of American Art.)

FIGURE 91. Photograph of the motif of Cézanne's La Sainte Victoire, Figure 92. (Courtesy, Erle Loran.)

FIGURE 92. La Sainte Victoire, by Paul Cézanne. Natural forms are here controlled and brought into a unity consistent with the flat picture plane. Background objects are strengthened and brought forward; foreground objects flattened and pushed back, giving both planes a more unified relation to each other and the whole surface. Compare with the original motif, Figure 91. (Courtesy, Erle Loran.)

mental interest in positive-negative space relationships to achieve the greatest possible tension on a two-dimensional surface. This is done by equalizing the positive and negative forces, usually bringing the negative areas to a position slightly less advancing than the positive ones.

The artist must constantly keep in mind when drawing or painting objects (whether they be human bodies, furniture, trees, mountains, or what not) that they are volumes to be arranged in relation to other volumes and negative spaces on the three-dimensional stage; that volumes are made of planes; that planes are made of patterns and tones, colors, lines, and textures; and that all the means must be dovetailed and fused into a totally unified, varied, and energized whole.

Because of the complexity of all these factors it can readily be understood why the intuitive senses must play the greater part in creating a work of art; an intuitive sense of rightness must be used in volume placement, space-interval timing, and coordination of all the forces into a form that is vital and complete.

8. THEME AND EXPRESSION

The theme, as we explained in an earlier chapter, is the psychological aspect of a picture—the topic, story, mood, or emotion expressed. It is, or should be, so infused and integrated with form and technique that all are one, inseparable and complete. The theme is the product of the form and technique; the form the result of the technique and theme. But for purposes of study, each of the three must be abstracted and separately analyzed.

The common mistake of the uneducated (perhaps "miseducated" is the correct term, because most humans have a natural inborn taste and intuitive sense with which to judge quality in the arts, unless it is debased by low standards of cultural environment and miseducation) the common mistake is to judge art works largely by the pretty sentiment of a story or theme. It is a mistake, as this whole book on art structure should make plain, because, above all, quality of form is the invariable constant in art.

We can say this because it is possible for an art work to exist in the abstract, decorative, or nonobjective state, totally without story or subject matter and still be vital and important; but having only a theme, without unity or design, it is not even worthy of being considered a work of art.

The nonobjective artist's position is that as long as beauty is a quality arriving out of abstract relationships of lines, colors, forms, and spaces, the way to achieve the purest beauty is to eliminate entirely any semblance of subjective material, thus making a work that is expressive of the purest objective reality. Of course, this argument is hard to refute, the only question being how much subjective truth one is prepared to give up for the sake of pure abstract beauty. This is a matter for personal decision.

Although subject matter is a part of most pictures, many people fail to take into consideration that it is merely one part and of little importance to the structural beauty of the form. For beauty is rather an abstract thing, a result of arbitrary elements in right relationship to one another. And while we might admit of thematic beauties, it must be remembered that these are only beauties when viewed by those having the correct background to consider them as such.

Ideas, sentimental values, and interpretations are continually changing, are never exactly the same in meaning from one generation to another or even from one individual to another. This is why we say that the theme is the psychological aspect. Each person reacts or responds differently to any given idea or emotion expressed, depending on his nature, his background, his experience, in short, his physiological and psychological makeup. An idea or object which is beautiful to one may be ugly to another because of differences in values of association. One person may go into hysterics upon seeing a mouse, while another may lovingly cherish one as a pet. One person may immediately develop choking spells and asthma upon seeing a bouquet of roses, even if they happen to be paper ones, while another will enjoy spending his life in the development and culture of this species of flower.

From the standpoint of abstract beauty nature is no respecter of persons or objects. With rare exceptions she lavishes each single organism (from an ant to a hippopotamus, an onion to a mountain peak, a snake to a sunset) with structural harmony and balance, in color and functional design. The idea that "the female human form is the most beautiful of nature's creations" was no doubt the subjective conclusion of a young male artist or philosopher. From a strictly abstract point of view there are no grounds for assuming that a woman is any more beautiful than a horse or an old gnarled tree.

Of course, all other things being equal (quality of form and technique) a good theme may be a most deciding weight in judging a work of art.

Because of the factor of individual psychology, though, it is hard to define a good theme exactly, unless we decide on the basis of wide acceptance or on moral grounds, and say that a theme is best which has the most universal appeal or which would have greatest effect for good over the longest period of time. By "moral," then, we do not necessarily mean a sweet or romantic moral preachment. A work may even be ugly or crude in a thematic sense and still give humanity a genuine push and lift upward (Fig. 95). It may be without literary meaning and divorced from storytelling altogether, be even abstract or completely nonfigurative, yet through its sheer beauty or symbolic form, be a force for moral uplift and spiritual refinement. These are moral values.

FIGURE 93. Arctic Thaw, by Paul Klee. Abstract symbols combined to depict a natural mood. (Courtesy, Nierendorf Gallery.)

It is the opinion of some that nonobjective works are, and can be, no more than exercises in design, frameworks for realistic pictures; but they can be more than that. They can be visual music or poetry with emotional and psychological meaning. They can even impress one with realistic ideas and moods by their aesthetic symbolism. The nonobjective field of expression is perhaps the least understood and the least developed of any in contemporary painting. Naturally an artist should have something to say as well as the ability to say it. But what he has to say may be of a more obscure, spiritual nature than shows on the surface, or he may have something to say about the geometrical beauty of nonrepresentational forms and ideas.

From the individual creator's point of view, any given theme is important to the extent that it moves him to strong and vital expression of his feelings or ideas about it. In this sense, theme may be considered as important as form, because it becomes a primary motivation toward the creation of a vital form and is an active element in the final result. In this same sense, technique can also become a definite and vital part in the forming of a whole art creation.

The combination of great form, vital theme, and technical excellence certainly spells *masterpiece* in any age. Giottos, Daumiers, Brueghels, Blakes, El Grecos, and Van Goghs are few and far between in the long history of art.

At present, we are in a period of form renaissance where many of the world's greatest creative artists are spending their energies and talents in design experimentation, as a reaction against the formless, emotionally dried-up, imitative expression of the eighteenth and nineteenth centuries.

At the beginning of the movement, this search for a more solid structural form was coupled with a reaction against literary and extra-sentimental subject matter, which had reached a point of romantic sweetness that was sickening to less vulgar minds.

The reaction against illustrational storytelling has led many artists into the fields of expressionism and surrealism, both of which depict ideas, moods, and

FIGURE 94. Composition, by Frank Bacher. An example of strict nonobjective painting. (Courtesy, the artist.)

emotions that lie beneath the physical surface and beyond oral description. This direction was given impetus by the development of the camera, which could record the outer visual aspects of nature with such perfect precision as to make it a waste of time and energy for the artist to attempt to compete with it.

These several factors in recent art history have influenced most artists to some extent, and many of those who have chosen to use subject material of the outer physical kind do so more directly through the artist's plastic means and with greater unity.

When nature studies are made, the student will do well to keep in mind the essential differences between the scientific and the artistic and approach the two accordingly. Working directly from nature can be disastrous to the creative talents, and while it is necessary to the development of a full rounded, mature artist, both instructor and student should be aware of the possible dangers.

The danger lies mostly in the attitude with which one approaches the subject, whether this attitude is creative or imitative. As an illustration, Robert Henri, outstanding American art teacher, in discussing this subject in relation to life drawing, said that if he had his way the model would pose in a different room

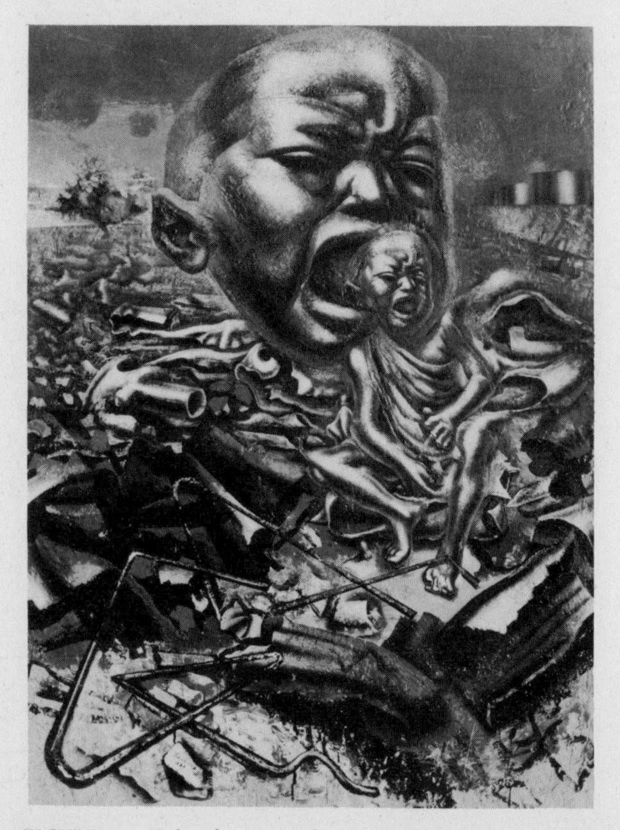

FIGURE 95. Echo of a Scream, by David Alfaro Siqueiros (Courtesy, Museum of Modern Art.)

from the one in which the students were working.

This would make the students think, feel, and interpret more and imitate less. It would make them study the basic structure and form of the model, get the knowledge more thoroughly in their minds before going back to their easel in the other room where they would be able to put down their learnings about the structure in a more direct manner. They would look at the model more as a means of thoughtful reference than as thoughtless imitation.

The difference between thoughtless looking and thoughtful seeing or knowing may be illustrated by citing an experiment carried out by the author with three groups of students, one blind and the other two normally sighted. A number of wooden forms were cut in the shape of cube, octagon, and sphere. These figures were camouflaged with a few simple color patterns and set before a group of twenty-one advanced students with the instruction that they were to draw the essential forms of what they saw as exactly as possible without getting nearer than ten feet to the models.

Not one of the twenty-one people really saw or interpreted the figures correctly. The basic forms of octagon, sphere, and the rest were completely lost in the students' efforts to copy the distracting camouflage patterns. The same models were given to a class of blind modeling students with the assignment of examining the figures (with the hands) and modeling the same things in clay. These students all got the essential shapes, and several were sensitive enough in their touch to feel the camouflage patterns and interpret them in the modeling.

Another group of eighteen beginning sighted students were given the assignment of interpreting the same models after examining them by touch in a dark room. Nearly all of these people got the essential shapes in their drawings, but not one was sensitive or thoughtful enough to realize the existence of the camouflage patterns on the forms. So the group of "blind" students won out over both of the sighted groups.

This experiment shows how little we can really learn by even thoughtful looking, let alone thoughtless imitation. Accordingly, everything possible should be done to stimulate an attitude of thoughtful and feelingful study, examination, theorizing, proving, disproving, and direct interpreting. Unessentials must be eliminated because they camouflage the basic form whenever the student works directly from nature —either in landscape, figure, or still life. This is the

FIGURE 96. The Starry Night, by Vincent Van Gogh. Dynamic line and pattern rhythms here act as symbols to express the artist's deeply felt reaction to a natural scene. (Collection, Museum of Modern Art.)

creative way for the true artist.

The dangers of working directly from nature are (1) the student may develop habits of thoughtless and feelingless imitation, and (2) he may learn so many scientific details about the subject that emotional and artistic freedom will be hampered or stifled.

On the other hand, in most cases there is danger in working altogether emotionally without some training in nature study. The results of this kind of overemphasis are shallowness, flamboyancy, overlooseness, and monotony.

One school of thought contends that the emotions should be freely exercised and full sway given to personal expression and individual taste, and that if any nature study is necessary, it should come later. An opposite view is taken by some who believe the emphasis should be placed first and foremost on studies from nature.

After much thought and experiment, it is the author's opinion that the two should be carried on simultaneously or intermittently but with greater proportion of time and emphasis on memory and imaginative exercises of the basic theories of design and form. At the same time, the two approaches should be kept clearly separated in the student's mind, and the difference stressed between the creative and imitative ways of working from nature. While the artist should not be too dependent on nature, he should at the same time remember that it is a continual well of inspiration, information, and form variation.

The problem of expressing ideas or moods of nature is sometimes simplified by deciding just what it is about a given subject that impresses us, what it is about the form or design that moves us to feel or think strongly about it. After learning what it is—the color, line, tone, space, or other relationship—we then emphasize this aspect, eliminating all that is superfluous to the thing we want to say.

As for subject material, the artist has a limitless choice of physical, emotional, and spiritual things and ideas. There are realistic, abstract, or emotional aspects of botany, geology, physics, economics, religion, politics, psychology, history, anatomy, human affairs and emotions, allegory, fantasy, geometry, form structure, and many more.

The amount of knowledge necessary concerning the content to be used depends upon the extent and type of form or emotion to be expressed—realism, symbolism, nonobjectivism, or other. To the realist, a thorough knowledge of anatomy, geology, or other sciences is indispensable, while to the abstractionist or emotional expressionist too much scientific accuracy would rather harm than help. However, if an artist is using any degree of natural subject at all, it is important to convey the spirit and mood of the subject depicted and a general emotional expression of the entirety.

Every object in nature has a character that is individual and distinct. The artist must uncover this inner spirit that hides beneath the outer shell of existing things, be they physically alive or dead as a rock. He must realize intellectually and emotionally this feeling and express it by elimination, reconstruction, and symbolism.

All natural forms have some type of vitality, whether they are organic or inorganic. A rock exists as a living form with spiritual vibration and dynamic relationship. In other words, a static thing, such as a tree stump, the ground, or a dead body, has dramatic possibilities for expression by the artist who is sensitive to the spirit or mood of these things. This inertness and stillness when dramatized become a sort of dynamic deadness in relation to more alive things. We might call it the action of inaction.

More obvious are the character and spirit of, let us say, a live human being, animal, or tree. The outward movements and actions are results of this spirit. Even the space between forms is full of the spirit of life. The play of this emotional action and counteraction between objects and spaces lends spiritual vitality, life, and meaning to the aggregate structure.

FIGURE 98. The Virgin with St. Inez and St. Tecla, by El Greco. Compare pattern variety and general design quality of this picture with similar subject, Figure 99. (Collection, National Gallery of Art, Mellon Collection.)

FIGURE 97. The Red Dress, by Gladys Rockmore Davis. (Courtesy Midtown Galleries.)

To catch the mood and temper of each object and figure, exaggerating and fusing it with a form and technique that help dramatize its spirit, is a most important objective of the expressionist. He feels deeply the mood of each form and action, making each line, tone, or other means shout the drama to the world. A pig will be so much a symbol of a pig that it will *stink!* A workman will *work!* A playing child will *play!* A tree will *dance with joy* or will *bend over in sorrow*, according to the mood to be expressed.

Mood is largely expressed in certain characteristic actions and movements. The mood of the aggregate structure depends on the timing and action of the assembled segments or units embodied in the synthesis. An integration of appropriate structural action with the particular theme and mood to be expressed—this is the artist's problem where theme and expression are concerned. He must feel the correct rhythmic timing and space interval between positive forms and negative areas and correlate it with the subject or mood at hand.

FIGURE 100. Combing Her Hair, by Isabel Bishop. A solidly formed, realistic figure, but as a design it is insensitive to two-dimensional space relationships. (Collection, Whitney Museum of American Art.)

FIGURE 99. Last Judgment, by Bernard Van Orley. Although the groups of figures here are placed within a strict design structure, the particular figures within these groups are monotonously placed and imitatively drawn. Compare with fine pattern and tone variation in Figure 98. (Courtesy, Metropolitan Museum of Art.)

The use of associative values is an important means of expressing given moods and ideas. Certain shapes, movements, and forces in nature are seen to exist under certain conditions and moods. Having seen these nature patterns in conjunction with certain moods many times since infancy, we accept them as symbols of these moods.

We have seen the calm lines of the horizon, a fallen tree, or reclining figure. The artist makes use of this design symbol by emphasizing horizontal lines in a composition where peace, quiet, and repose is the aim. We have seen and felt the dynamic movement of trees, grass, or other objects in a strong wind or storm. Diagonal lines transfer this emotional symbol to the canvas when powerful movement, action, and life are to be expressed. Graceful curves like those in the female body, rolling hills, or young trees are symbols of youth, playfulness, and harmony. Broken, jagged lines suggest lightning, anger, and excitement. Upright lines symbolize stability and austerity. Pyramidal lines give the feeling of monumentality, endurance, and strength. These are a few of the most obvious linear symbols taken from nature.

A key to symbolical expression is the human body itself. The difference between human emotions such as sadness, gayety, or hate may be studied in the various outward attitudes of the human body in such moods, and transferred to objects, animals, landscapes, or what not. The action of the human body in a lyrical dance, as an illustration, may be transferred to trees, clouds, or other landscape objects, imbuing them with the same expressive spirit.

Color, we may say, is the combination and sum total of all the other structural elements. So when we talk of its various functions the same may be applied to line, tone, and space, which it contains. As with the other means, there are two ways in which color may be said to function. They are form and expression.

Form would include all the ways in which color functions in attaining unity and plastic coordination by way of the principles of design. Under expression could be placed all the ways in which color may be used to more fully express ideas, realities, moods, or images.

Color symbols may represent the many things that an artist may choose to depict: the outer visual aspects, the unseen forces of nature, the inner emotions, the subconscious dreams, the moods and ideas of imagination, and the rest. The creative artist searches for symbols that represent these things, inventing color shapes, planes, and combinations of all his legitimate means, molding them into a form that makes of his emotions, concepts, and thoughts a concrete reality.

Color, tone, space, and texture symbols can be found in nature for the artist's use in expressing ideas and moods. Chords of analogous colors in light yellows, greens, and blues symbolize spring, youth, and ecstasy, coinciding with graceful linear rhythms, light tone-value harmonies, and flowing space patterns. Blue-greens, blues, and violets in combination suggest coldness, winter, and the like. Harmonies of modified reds, oranges, and yellows bring to mind autumn, evening, and old age.

FIGURE 101. Winter Twilight, by Max Weber. An example of expressionism. (Courtesy, Santa Barbara Museum, Hammett Collection.)

Tone-value harmonies in low key remind one of night, eeriness, and romance. Strong contrasts of tone, color, or space say opposition, war, abruptness, and discord. Certain form and space combinations have symbolical meaning to us. Upward reaching arches and pinnacles are remindful of religion, faith, and high purpose. Inverted arches mean the opposite—oppression, sadness, and weariness.

Upward flamelike forms suggest burning ambition, spiritual intensity, and aspiration. There are many other symbols and countless combinations of them in nature for the artist's expressive needs. Certain types of movement within the three dimensions of the pictorial stage—points and counterpoints, rhythms, oppositions, variations in timing of pictorial action—

FIGURE 102. Expressive line symbols. 1. bending upright line, suggesting sadness, weariness, grief. 2. upward swirls, suggesting aspiration, spiritual intensity, ardor. 3. rhythmic horizontals, suggesting laziness, sleepiness, joyous calm. 4. upward spray, suggesting growth, idealism, spontaneity. 5. diminishing perspective, suggesting distance, limited expanse, nostalgia. 6. inverted perspective, suggesting infinite expanse, expanding space, unhampered freedom. 7. waterfall, suggesting gravity, rhythmic descent. 8. concentric arcs, suggesting upward expansion, flowering movement, buoyancy. 9. horizontal line, suggesting tranquillity, repose, immobility. 10. verticals, suggesting stability, austerity, dignity. 11. rounded arches, suggesting strength, heavy austerity. 12. diagonals, suggesting instability, movement, action. 13. pyramid, suggesting stability, dignity, massive strength. 14. Gothic arch, suggesting spiritual uplift, faith, religious hope. 15. rhythmic curves, suggesting grace, joyousness, youth. 16. spiral line, suggesting genesis, generative forces. 17. expanding spheres, suggesting slow buoyancy, good spirits, phantasy. 18. conflicting diagonals, suggesting war, conflict, hate, confusion. 19. zig-zag line, suggesting excitement, jagged animation. 20. radiation lines, suggesting concentration, explosion, sudden outburst.

depict certain moods in painting as in music.

Unity of expression demands singleness of purpose and simplification of expression. Too many moods in one picture add confusion and disunity, to put it another way. A dominant theme and mood with subordinate features is a rule that works here, as in all places where unity is desired.

The painter's communicative instruments are essentially those of color planes and symbols. Through these he is able to utter messages of physical, mental, or emotional reality. There are various schools of thought as to the legitimacy of each of these, many claiming that pictures which attempt to portray mental ideas and physical appearances of nature infringe on the essential field of literature or drama. Too often this is the case. It is true that each of the arts has a peculiar means of communication and each should function by its own natural technique.

FIGURE 103. Sleeping, by John Carroll. (Courtesy, New York Graphic Society.)

FIGURE 104. Analysis of Figure 103. Soft, floating patterns in horizontal direction symbolize calm, restful mood as in sleep.

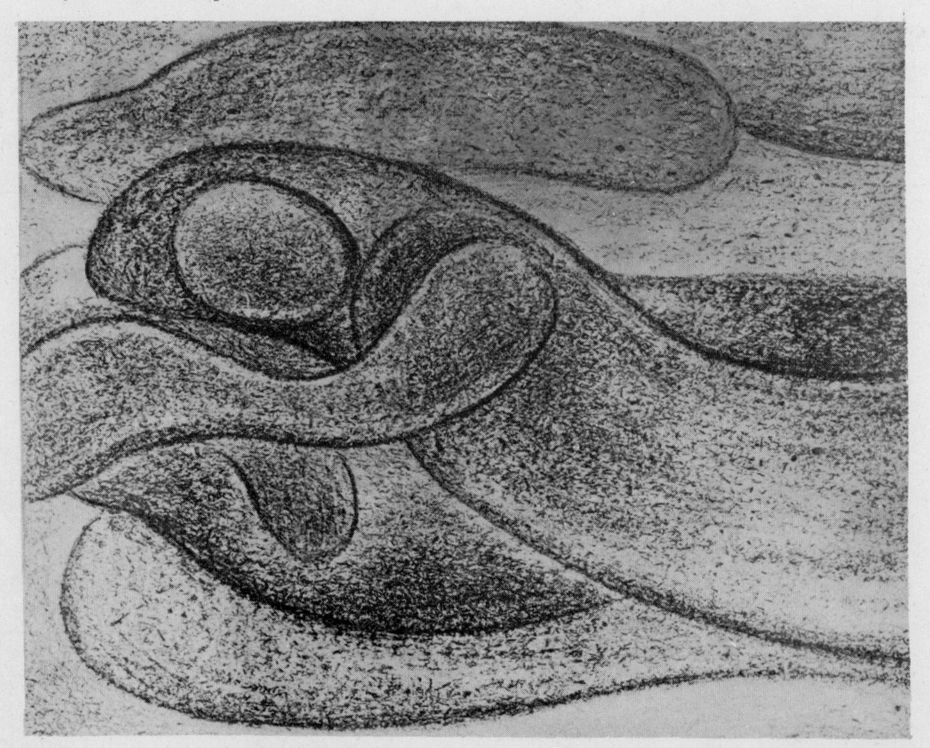

FIGURE 105. Tornado, by Mario Carreño. Diagonal lines, depicting dynamic action. (Collection, Museum of Modern Art.)

FIGURE 106. Desolation, by Raquel Forner. An illustration of human actions transferred to a landscape subject. (Collection, Museum of Modern Art.)

FIGURE 107. Panel from border of screen, by Fong Long Kong of Fatsam (early Chinese). Characteristic movement of various objects, symbolizing different moods. (Collection, Metropolitan Museum of Art.)

For expressing his own feelings and thoughts about life, nature, or other considerations, the artist's rightful purpose is to find *plastic* equivalents or symbols that parallel his personal emotions and reactions to a given scene or idea. The original scene may be one of physical reality and the artist's reaction may be largely mental; but if the result of his reactions is told only in terms of literary descriptions, then he should make his statement in words rather than in paint or marble. The point is that the painter or sculptor should speak in terms of his special medium with planes and symbols, whether his subject be physical, mental, or emotional. Sometimes his symbol for a given thing may be quite like the actual appearance of the natural motif, which is legitimate as long as it is arrived at through honest use of the artist's plastic means. But if it is arrived at through the channels of literature, that is, merely through sentiment and storytelling, depicting objects and things primarily by way of literary descriptions and mental ideas, then the expression is dishonest and illegitimate as far as the arts of painting or sculpture are concerned.

The work shown in Fig. 108, and the following text which accompanies it in the guide book from which it was taken, illustrates a complete lack of unity between the subject and the sculptor's plastic means. As the explanation proves, the work is based altogether on literary and sentimental values and is not a piece of sculptural art but a story illustrated in stone.*

Normally there is little physical difference if any in the way each artist sees nature. But there is a great deal of difference in the way each is capable of seeing or chooses to see nature in the mind's eye. This is what is meant by the saying, "each artist sees nature in a different way."

In respect to this matter of personal interpretation, it is interesting to note that in analyzing and diagraming a work of art, the same creative process is used that the creative artist uses in interpreting nature. In order to clarify the thing he wishes to say concerning his feelings or ideas of the thing at hand, he extracts certain things, recreates, dramatizes, simplifies, diagrams, and symbolizes them. The quality of the resultant expression depends upon this inner vision, coupled with the ability to interpret it in a unified way so that others may clearly perceive the idea or emotion in mind. The lack of this quality is one of the reasons that the uncreative, imitative worker in any of the arts

THE STORY OF THE MYSTERY OF LIFE

as one person interprets it

Around the mystic Stream of Life we see grouped eighteen persons typifying many walks and stations in life. First we see

1, a boy, who is astonished at the miracle that has happened in his hand—one moment, an unbroken egg; the next moment, a chick, teeming with life. "Why?" he asks. "How does it happen? What is the answer to this Mystery of Life?" He questions

2, his aged grandmother, who, he reasons, knows everything. But we see her resigned in the face of the inexplicable. Then we see

3 & 4, the lovers, who believe they have found the answer to the mystery in their first kiss;

5, the sweet girl graduate, lost in dreams, with no place as yet in her thoughts for a serious questioning of Life's destiny;

6, the scientist, troubled because all his learnings, all his searchings, have not solved the mystery;

7 & 8, the mother, who finds the answer in the babe at her breast;

9, 10, 11, 12, 13, the happy family group, not greatly perturbed by the mystery, although even they seem to ask: "Why do the doves mate?"

14, the learned philosopher, scratching his puzzled head in vain;

15 & 16, the monk and the nun, comforted and secure, confident that they have found the answer in their religion;

17, the atheist, the fool, who grinningly cares not at all, while

18, the stoic, sits in silent awe and contemplation of that which he believes he knows but cannot explain or understand.

Gentle Reader, what is *your* interpretation? Do you see yourself in one of the characters here portrayed? Forest Lawn has found the answer to the Mystery of Life. Have you found it? Or are you still in anxious doubt?

* Reprinted from the *Art Guide of Forest Lawn*, courtesy of Forest Lawn Memorial-Park, Glendale, California.

FIGURE 108. *The Mystery of Life, by Ernesto Gazzeri. An example of the literary approach in sculpture. Total lack of plastic design and coordination. Emphasis placed on sentimental storytelling by way of literary ideas and surface details rather than through sculpture's natural plastic means. (Courtesy, Forest Lawn Memorial Park.)*

FIGURE 109. *Pietà, by Charles Umlauf. Deep dramatic expression told in honest sculptural terms. (Courtesy, the artist.)*

cannot be accepted seriously as a true artist, for as we have said elsewhere, imitation does not express anything. It merely transfers a view or parts of it from one place to another.

It is a fact that every great artist from the most ancient to the most modern has changed the normal proportions and general photo-exact likeness of nature to some greater or lesser extent for reasons of expression or design. There are dramatic effects that can be achieved in no other way. The comic strip and movie cartoon are examples of this distortion of fact for purposes of dramatic expression. One can easily imagine how lacking in drama and emphasis either would be if these caricatures were replaced with factual proportions and doings. Distortion of natural facts works the same way in the more serious picture.

The plastic and graphic artist has need for poetic license no less than the poet. As pointed out before, the extent of the use of this license is an individual problem and may vary from artist to artist or even from picture to picture by the same artist, depending on the need or purpose of the expression in each case.

Artistic talent depends to a great degree on two things: form, the ability to organize; and expression, the ability to feel intensely. This leads to a logical and important conclusion on the subject of theme and expression—that the artist, in order to interpret the mood and spirit of a thing, must first feel profoundly that spirit. In order to feel profoundly he must have swum deeply in the sea of life.

9. TECHNIQUE

While the subject of technique is rather outside the realm of this study, we shall touch on a few points that have a bearing on the things we are concerned with here.

To serve our purpose we may break down the general subject into three simple divisions. These we will call *quality*, *permanency*, and *function*.

By quality we mean largely the aesthetic excellence to be attained by the use of certain materials, tools, and methods of application.

There is no doubt that the general aesthetic beauty and expressive worth of any work are greatly enhanced by the use of fine materials and masterful execution. In the latter we are not referring to a slickness or overly clever application in style or method, but rather the opposite. For instance, lines and space patterns become more characterful when they are applied with feeling and sensitiveness and are marked with variation in width, texture, tone, and accent, thus becoming masterful in quality and character.

This feeling for variation is ofttimes lost in those with academic or conventional art training, while in many unschooled artists and children the quality is seen at its best.

One must continually guard against an overconventionalization of the means—lines, spaces, colors, and the rest—and avoid stereotyped, mannered effects that might be called hackneyed or trite, effects which in writing would suggest the term "cliché." A thing need not be pretty to be beautiful. Mere prettiness is a weakness. Character is the thing to be sought after. Homeliness, naïveté, or even crudity may be excused if the work shows sincerity and character.

The key to technical quality is usually to be found in the material itself. One merely has to develop a sensitiveness to it. When water colors are used, as a case in point, many interesting variations take place in accidental ways merely because of the essential watery character of the medium. If one learns to take advantage of these accidents and coaxes the pigment along in the general direction in which one is headed rather than forcing it, the end result will be both more beautiful and expressive. One must develop the attitude of give and take, letting the material have a chance to decide its own direction at times, while one develops a sensitive feeling as to right relationships and effects.

Each medium—oil, tempera, gouache, ink, charcoal, or other, as well as the canvas, paper, or surface on which the medium is applied—has certain intrinsic qualities and characteristics with which the artist should become acquainted and of which he should take advantage.

Certain strictly technical ways of handling materials

FIGURE 110. Drawing by Donna Rasmusen. A free calligraphic expression by a five-year-old child.

FIGURE 111. Drawings for furniture, by Thomas Chippendale. Overstylized, imitative, non-functional "design." (Collection, Metropolitan Museum of Art.)

FIGURE 112. Indian Door to Senate Chamber, Nebraska State Capitol Building, by Lee Lawrie. Pseudo-modern sculpture. Hackneyed and monotonous over-ornamentation. (Courtesy, J. H. Jansen, Publishers.)

FIGURE 113. Le Chahut, by Georges Seurat. An example of broken color (pointillism). (Courtesy, Albright Art Gallery.)

add to the design enrichment and expression, such as various ways of applying color to the canvas, like glazing, scumbling, dry brush, heavy pigment, broken color, and many more. Interesting and unusual effects are possible by experimenting with various tools like comb, palette knife, tooth brush, fingers, sponge, or burlap.

The broken-color technique, or what is sometimes called color scintillation or pointillism, is of enough importance to warrant mentioning it here. It is based on the principle that all colors are derived from the three primaries, red, yellow, and blue. Therefore, the theory goes, in order to arrive at any certain color one needs merely to apply little spots of the component colors side by side on the canvas rather than mixing them together on the palette—letting the eyes of the viewer, standing at some distance from the picture where the colors seem to merge, do the mixing. The effect is that of atmosphere and light, adding richness and looseness to the painting. In nature there are different degrees of scintillation according to the amount of light at a given moment. A low scintillation can be arrived at by mixing colors in close analogy or by using more modified (grayer) colors. The vibration can be raised by mixing colors farther away from each other in the scale and also by adding their mutual complementary.

While most of the original pointillists used the three primaries and three secondaries—six colors in all—and stuck to a rather strict and sometimes mechanical use of the theory, one can use it less formally to fit one's own purposes and desires, breaking the color and texture by using lines, smudges, blendings, and so on.

Color luminosity and richness can be gained by the method called *glazing*, which consists of applying several coats of transparent paint (thinned with oil or varnish) over each other after a thorough drying of each coat. Many of the old masters used this method. Outstanding among them are Rembrandt, Rubens, Brueghel, and Titian.

Many contemporary artists prefer a more direct, opaque technique, sometimes applying pigments over each other semiopaquely in smudge or dry-brush fashion. This is called *scumbling*.

These and many other methods are problems for personal experimentation, each artist developing a

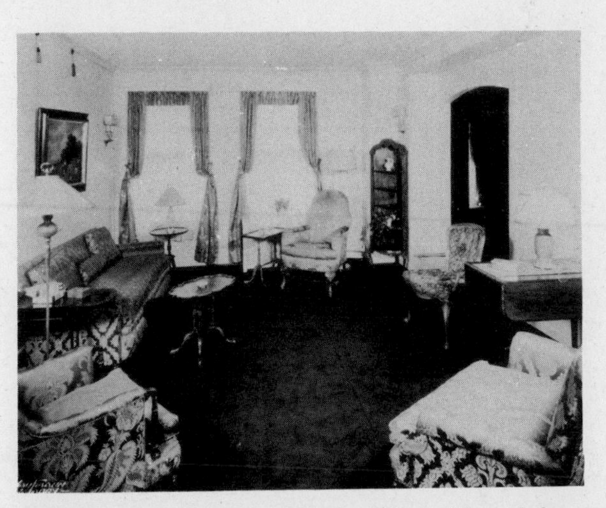

FIGURE 114A. A room of the Shoreland Hotel, Chicago, before redecoration.

FIGURE 114B. The same room as 114A, after redecoration

FIGURE 115. Prometheus, mural, by José Clemente Orozco. (Courtesy, Pomona College, Claremont, California.)

technique suitable to his individual style and needs.

On permanency we shall not even touch, it being so strictly a technical subject outside the field of aesthetic design, and there being so many good books that consider the problem thoroughly and scientifically. We might only say in passing that permanency is of great importance in retaining any art work of aesthetic merit for future generations, and that one should make a habit of using the finest materials possible, for the sake of both quality and permanency.

Function is the application of a thing to certain purposes. Putting it more precisely, it is the designing of a work in terms of the particular medium employed and the particular use to which it will be applied.

In spite of a general renaissance in this direction, we are still surrounded by arts and crafts, architecture, and industrial products that are neither designed in terms of the media used nor for the use to which they are to be put. We still find architects imitating Greek temples and medieval Gothic cathedrals in an age of concrete and steel—in a modern civilization completely foreign to anything of the past in mood and tempo. We still see gas heaters designed to look like fire logs, jewelry to look like ribbon and lace, flower holders to look like horns of plenty, and wallpaper to look like a garden of flowers and leaves. We see murals that are merely enlarged easel pictures where the ideas would be better expressed in writing, and we see sculptured decorations for architecture that are neither architectural nor sculptural.

On the credit side, we do find some functional and, as a result, beautiful refrigerators, automobiles, airplanes, and other industrial products for everyday use.

The artist must be conscious of the form and material in relation to the function. The sculptor should decide whether wood, bronze, or stone would best suit the needs of his particular problem and design it in harmony with its eventual environment. An outdoor piece would be seen in a different perspective and different lighting from one indoors, and also be subjected to various changes in the weather. A theme light in nature, which may work out very well as a small bronze to be placed on a table, may be entirely unsuited in medium, theme, handling, or scale as a large piece of garden sculpture or architectural note.

Few easel pictures, no matter how excellent in quality, would look right as mural decorations either as to scale or design. Each mural space is a unique problem, and the artist needs to consider the design and color in relation to the architecture, the scale, and the function of the building itself.

Aside from these considerations of functional unity, the most blatant fault of many murals is a violation of the flat nature of the wall on which they are placed. Figures or other objects fall forward past the front picture plane; naturalistic perspective takes the eye far into distant places; holes are recessed through the back plane because of a lack of volume, color, or textural foils. Essential wall flatness is best retained, the same as in easel painting, by limiting the total depth to a shallow range and flattening all forms to a bas-relief effect or, when using stronger, full rounded forms, by arranging them close to the front plane, reversing areal and lineal perspective, modifying the forms with subdued coloring, and filling background holes with corrective colors, forms, tones, or textures.

One or more good books on the subject of technique are an indispensable part of the artist's equipment. Several of these are included in the supplementary reading list at the back of this book.

10. ANALYSIS OF *The Wedding Dance*

After analyzing the several means and the laws of unity and seeing how they work in various pieces of sculpture and painting, it seemed advisable to take one art work and make a more or less complete analysis of it as a review of all the primary points concerned.

It was no easy matter to find such a piece—one that would embody most of the principles outlined, all integrated and more or less complete; one that would illustrate masterful design, great theme, and superb technique. For our purposes Brueghel's *The Wedding Dance* seemed to be a most suitable choice.

Each of the isolated means will first be considered in the analysis, and later all of them in sum total, following the general method of the book.

THE CREATIVE ATTITUDE

A most cursory study of *The Wedding Dance* will show that it is creative and not imitative. Although a realistic scene with people and objects of more or less natural appearances is depicted, the artist was creative in designing each segment and the whole. Natural contours are reshaped for purposes of greater dramatic expression, characterization, and variation. Notice in the detail (Fig. 117) how the size of the shoulders and arms of the dancer at the left is exaggerated in comparison with his legs; how the total contour is simplified and made into an interesting pattern; and how the mood of *dance* is dramatized by the exaggerated curve of his body and the angle of his knees. Notice these same things in the figure of the woman with whom he is dancing—the carefully felt pattern contours of shoulders, costume, and foot, the rhythmic lines in her hat and dress that add to the particular jumping motion that is her part in the dance.

Other creative aspects of this painting will be brought out as its structure is studied, showing how the natural objects are reshaped, placed, and molded into the net plastic expression.

TWO-DIMENSIONAL LINE

The linear surface structure in *The Wedding Dance* is secondary, as is usual for this type of work which places emphasis on the arrangement of volumes in third-dimensional space. For this reason the following analysis may seem exaggerated, but the author believes that although it is hidden and subordinated by the more important three-dimensional masses (Figs. 123 and 124), the line pattern as seen in Fig. 118 is essentially true. The larger masses are arranged in a symmetrical design of circles stabilized by a number of straight lines running diagonally across the two-dimensional field. In keeping with the general usage of diminishing perspective in the picture, the circles are larger in the front and smaller as they move toward the rear. The vertical lines of trees and other objects at the rear add an advancing textural pattern, helping to hold the background in relation to the flat picture plane. The horizontal lines at top and bottom help to stabilize the circles and diagonal lines and relate the total form to the top and bottom of the format or frame.

While the large lineal structure is rather mechanical, the various figures which go to make up the masses these lines describe are loosely active and rhythmical, almost hiding the main structure from view. In certain instances we might find fault with this design, as in the most obvious circle on the right which forms the curve of the roof and the black-coated figure in the middle distance below. In this case, the figure belongs to one mass and his coat to another; this develops an optical illusion depending on which mass one happens to be focusing one's attention on. There are a number of such spots in the picture where form is not completely integrated with line, but on the whole the lineal structure ties in very well.

PATTERN (TWO-DIMENSIONAL SPACE)

The single objects in the picture are simple and attractive in their general contour shapes. Even in the secondary parts of each figure this may be seen (Fig. 119). These shapes are not as varied or as related as in a more modern work, such as an abstraction by Picasso (Fig. 6), Braque, or Gris, but considering the necessary compromise with realism in a work

FIGURE 116. *The* **Wedding** *Dance, by Pieter Brueghel the Elder.* (*Courtesy, Detroit Institute of Arts.*)

of this kind, the contours are surprisingly good. Few of the Italian pictures of about this time show as much concern for pattern, and on this count most of them are quite weak. Later painters, like Van Dyck and Rubens, showed even less interest in contour variation, placing most of the emphasis on overlapping volume and rhythmic line.

The detail (Fig. 117) shows how irrelevant details have been eliminated and contours changed from the natural likenesses for reasons of subject dramatization and pattern interest. Contour lines are drawn in long, simple strokes with interior forms subordinated and the emphasis placed on the outer edges. All the patterns are closed.

The negative areas around the figures in *The Wedding Dance* are not considered to be spacial shapes as are the positive areas, which is usual in realistic works of this kind. In this case the positive shapes take up so much space, leaving little room for the negative areas, that this may not be considered an important lack.

In regard to space relation and coordination, there are a few places where static points are found, such as

FIGURE 117. Detail of The Wedding Dance.

where the coat of the dancing figure in the right foreground touches the folds of the dress on the woman at his right. However, such spots are few and quite negligible in relation to the fine coordination and rhythm of the whole. The left side of the painting shows a better relation of positive and negative areas, the right background being rather confused because of a lack of massing of the figure groups.

TWO-DIMENSIONAL TONE

A light medium tone is most dominant in the allover tonal scheme of *The Wedding Dance*, with a dark medium tone second in size of area consumed. Upon this background of medium tones are decoratively scattered the black and white tones which more or less hold the tonal scheme together. With some imagination the black tones can be seen to form triangular-shaped areas, mostly across the middle distance. The white tones show little massing but instead are repeated as small spots in a large oval at the center of the design.

Within the single units of the picture the tones are massed quite simply, there being in most cases only

FIGURE 118. Structural line analysis of The Wedding Dance.

slight changes toward light or dark for purposes of drawing out the form. This tonal simplicity within the single figures contributes to the greatness of Brueghel's form, and it is especially important because of the complexity which is typical of his work.

TWO-DIMENSIONAL COLOR

The dominant color in the picture is yellow ochre,

FIGURE 119. Diagram of some space patterns found in The Wedding Dance, illustrating their simplicity and variety.

and it saturates and modifies all the other colors in the design. In the ground areas it goes toward green, in the trees and ground shadows toward brown, with some part of most of the people's costumes being pure ochre. Small areas of bright vermilion, light blue, eggshell white, and warm black are decoratively spotted over the entire area where the figures are.

The vermilion is the only more or less intense color used in *The Wedding Dance*, the other colors being quite low in key. The whites are intense because of their high tone value in contrast to the blacks and other tones of medium range.

The general color scheme of the picture is analogous, the dominant hue (as mentioned above) being yellow, and the other colors going toward yellow-green on one side in the color wheel and toward vermilion (yellow-red) on the other. The cool light blues act as a mutual complement to the yellows, giving balance to the two-dimensional color design.

TEXTURE

Texture in the modern sense is practically nonexistent in the painting with the exception of slight variations in the costumes where folds are used in contrast to the simple flatness of the others, or where the natural texture of the grass contrasts with the smoother areas.

FIGURE 120. Simplified diagram of tone values in The Wedding Dance.

THIRD-DIMENSIONAL LINE

The three-dimensional line movement is probably the most important cohesive factor in the structure of *The Wedding Dance*. The initial thrust into the field begins on the left side (Fig. 121), pushes in a direct curve into the background, goes across and returns to the middle of the field, where it moves in and is diffused. Two other secondary movements begin on the front plane at the center and at the right. They move into the middle distance in rhythm with the major drive, the one in the center developing a spiral which becomes the picture's focal point.

Within these big structural movements there are strong minor ones developed by the actions of the various figures (small arrows, Fig. 121). These are most active around the focal point made up of the dancing group in the near center of the design.

FIGURE 121. Diagram of the third-dimensional pictorial movement in The Wedding Dance.

THIRD-DIMENSIONAL SPACE

The diminishing size of the space patterns as they move toward the rear gives a deep third-dimensional form to *The Wedding Dance*. This perspective thrust is held in check by the wall of trees and the reverse perspective of the color, tone, and other means.

The space intervals between positive forms in the inward-outward thrusts are rather erratic and hit and miss. This is compensated for to some extent by the color and tone intervals which show better timing.

THIRD-DIMENSIONAL TONE

Instead of being modified as they recede, the tones in the picture are arbitrarily spotted over the whole picture regardless of the distance plane on which they are found (Fig. 116); that is, the blacks are just as dark in the background as in the foreground, the whites are just as light, and other tones the same. This is extremely important because it helps to limit the recession and bring the total form into a more static direction in relation to the picture plane.

The repetition of each tone from form to form in and out of the picture field is varied in space interval.

The black acts more or less as a cohesive agent that holds the various figure groups together because it is massed in larger areas (Fig. 120). The whites, being placed in smaller repeated spots, lead the eye through the three-dimensional space and are closely integrated with the lineal movements as diagramed in Fig. 121.

THIRD-DIMENSIONAL COLOR

Color in *The Wedding Dance* is used decoratively rather than plastically; that is, it works in the same way as does the tone-value means as described above—the same hues in the same intensities are used in the background objects as in those on the front plane. This is an arbitrary and creative use of color and tone, for it reverses the scientific laws of perspective in regard to these means.

Covering the receding volumes with intense color in this way, brings them forward and accentuates the natural flatness of the two-dimensional picture plane.

THIRD-DIMENSIONAL TEXTURE

As pointed out in a previous paragraph, texture plays little part in the two-dimensional design of the painting. But regarding the third dimension, it plays an important role in the same way as do color and tone in advancing the back planes toward a greater two-dimensional surface.

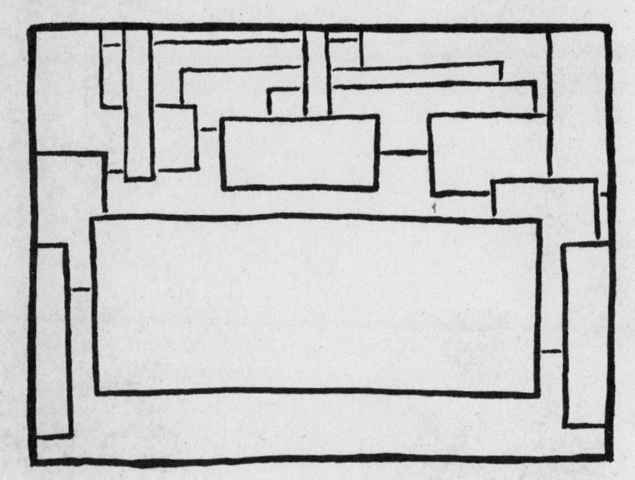

FIGURE 122. Simplified diagram of distance planes in The Wedding Dance.

As we said, there is little tactile variation in the surface quality of the various forms. But if one considers the whole design at once, it can be seen that the profusion of the small patterns on the back plane are in contrast to the simple ones in the front. Thus the complexity or general activity of the mass in the rear makes it more advancing in relation to the textural quietness of the nearer mass.

TWO-DIMENSIONAL PLANES

Figure 121 is an exaggerated diagram of the distance-plane arrangement in *The Wedding Dance*. Following the general lineal outline of the picture, these planes are balanced from side to side in a symmetrical design. The movement follows the overlapped planes around the outer edges of the field, returning to the large plane in front which is the focal point because of its dominant size.

By studying this diagram in conjunction with that in Fig. 121, it can be clearly seen how Brueghel held the back field in check by interlacing the planes with the trees in a horizontal movement across this area.

FIGURE 123. Simplified diagram of the volume arrangement in The Wedding Dance.

DIRECTIONAL PLANES AND VOLUMES

As is illustrated in Fig. 123, the upright planes that go to make up the volume masses in the painting are dominantly parallel to the picture plane. The large mass in front has an over-all flatness in this sense and the other planes work in a half circle around the back of this. The large trees in the middle distance add to this static plane design.

By comparing this diagram of volume arrangement (Fig. 123) with the photograph of the original picture, it can be seen how Brueghel has tipped the top planes upward, to bring them also into a more nearly parallel relation to the picture plane.

The same thing is true of the general ground plane which is pushed in at the bottom of the picture and tipped forward at the rear. This tipping of the plane gives the effect of the artist's viewing it from above, while the figures themselves do not, thus bringing the ground and the figures into closer parallel relation, and into a more static relation to the picture plane.

The center of interest in the picture is the group of dancing figures in the foreground. A focal point is created here in several ways, by the active lineal movement, the detail in the drawing, and so on, but largely by the dominant size of the figures and the whole volume mass. The weight and activity of this mass give it the importance of a fulcrum which balances the most distant forms.

Usually the focal point is seen to be closer to the center of the field, but here it is quite near to the front plane. In the original painting there is a line across the close foreground just below the feet of the figures, which leads to the conclusion that an extra section was added here after the picture was started in order to shift the focal point farther back into the field. There are other break lines in the painting, but they seem to be natural contractions of the panel while the

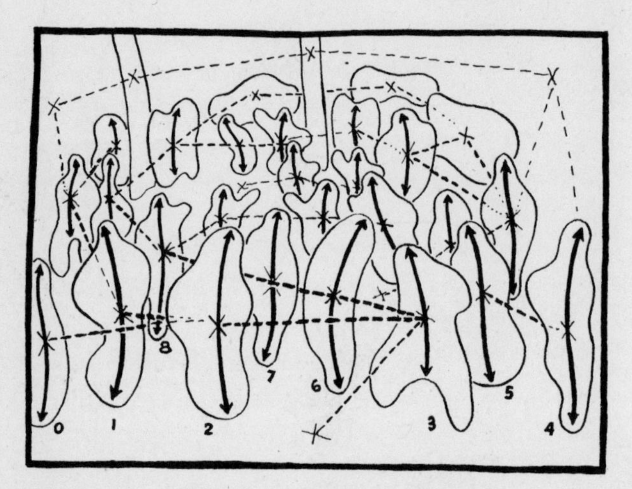

FIGURE 124. Diagram of the tensions between planes in The Wedding Dance.

one in the foreground shows retouching and a conscious effort to cover the line where the new section was added.

VOLUME TENSIONS

Figure 124 explains the important tensions in *The Wedding Dance*. It shows how the several means already considered all combine to develop tensions and movements in the total space.

Figure 3 holds the most important position because of its dynamic relation to the ground plane and the figures nearby. Figures 0, 1, and 2 are perhaps next in tensional activity, 1 and 2 being the most active of the three. Another tension between 4 and 5 on the other side creates a movement which balances these. Figure 3 gains much of its importance from the fact that it is the point of initial movement into space and its dynamic relation to the ground, and figures 1 and 2 to the left balance and stabilize the movement of the general total form. The tensions between the axes of the trees and other background forms make a movement across the top of the picture which repeats the movement across the front plane, giving unity to the general movement in relation to the limits of the field.

THEME AND EXPRESSION

The subject content of *The Wedding Dance* is of particular and permanent interest, one that could be termed a universal theme.

The subject is well integrated with the form, the general movement of the main drives carrying an expressive tempo which gives plastic form to the theme. The single units (figures) are extremely active in expressing the dance and the other moods of gayety and interest coincident with such an occasion. Each person is seen to be dramatically active in portraying his own particular mood or part in the scheme.

Brueghel had a profound understanding of humans in their happier moods and stated these things in a wholesome and realistic manner. His knowledge of human attitudes and expressions can be seen by studying the individual characters in this painting, each of which is a dramatic portrait of a characteristic type. The action of each figure coincides with the essential character of his features and general appearance.

The general color and tonal scheme of the painting also have a part in expressing the gayety of the scene, but line is the major expressive plastic means. This is most obvious in the dancing figures, the lilting rhythms of their bodies and limbs being the central motif in the design.

TECHNIQUE

The original of *The Wedding Dance* is painted in a mixed technique (tempera with oil or varnish glazes) on a wooden panel. The craftsmanship is superb. With age, the glazes have taken on added transparency, giving the picture a high luminosity that makes it sparkle like a rare jewel.

In response to an inquiry addressed to the Detroit Institute of Arts about the painting, the following information was received, which we quote verbatim:

> Our painting of *The Wedding Dance* by Brueghel turned up in an English private collection a little less than twenty years ago and was purchased by Dr. Valentiner who happened to be in London at the time the picture came on the English art market. It was known that Pieter Brueghel had executed such a picture for there were a number of old copies in existence in Berlin, Bath, Balti-

more, Sacramento, and elsewhere. The Antwerp Museum a few years before had purchased a very good copy which they believed to be the original until ours appeared. It has now been accepted by the Antwerp Museum that theirs is a copy after ours. The large number of copies executed in the generation after Brueghel's death shows how popular the picture must have been in its own time.

The paint has grown translucent with age so that one can follow the artist's process of production remarkably well. The picture is on a panel which has a gesso coating. The design follows a rough tracing in black. The tracing might be in some places ink applied with a quill, but in other places it looks very much like black chalk drawing. The paint is oil applied partly in glazes and partly in hatching strokes of impasto. In some places where the light dominates the paint is creamy and thick, modeling the form, in others it shades into glazes in the shadowed parts. One can see that the final contours do not always follow the drawing on the gesso, but the artist made corrections and changes. Many pentimenti are visible in the paint itself following the artist's changes. The use of short, rather nervous brushstrokes of a small single brush combined with glazes is characteristic throughout. It is curious that the many small brushstrokes should, at a distance, melt into a harmonious whole almost as firm as the effect of a Fifteenth Century Flemish painting with its even, smooth, enamel like paint. The picture is dated at the lower right 1566.

11. CONCLUSION

Out of the thousands of pictures painted each year not many will outlast their makers, and of those that do only an exceptional few, if any, will merit the term *great* and eventually through the test of time be called *masterpieces*. Those that really deserve such rating will no doubt do so because of certain basic principles of design and expression which time has proved to be traditional and constant. These principles, we may say, are universal.

It is possible in a general way to set down the rules of the universal tradition by which art works stand or fall. These positive principles we have attempted to cover essentially, if not in detail, in the greater part of the book. A few words from the negative point of view in relation to contemporary art may help clarify the subject and be useful in a short summing up.

FIGURE 125. The Meeting of St. Anthony and St. Paul, by Sassetta. (Collection, National Gallery of Art, Kress Collection.)

The majority of works of today, just as those of yesterday and tomorrow, will probably fall down on one or more of the following points: (1) lack of creative approach; (2) lack of order and design; (3) lack of expressive meaning; (4) lack of taste and sincerity; (5) lack of originality; (6) lack of imagination.

All six of the lacks are more or less intertwined. Each is dependent on the others. Expressive meaning results partly from the plan or design of the original motive and partly from being original, which depends partly on the taste of the artist. So in order to gain expressive meaning, in order to say something about his personal mental or emotional reaction to the subject, the artist's creative vision and imagination must be active and tasteful, redesigning, recreating nature, or inventing symbols or images that represent his individual feelings about the things he experiences by way of sight, smell, touch, intuition, or other channels.

Concerning lack of creative approach, as we have said before in different words, the painter who copies nature is merely a parrot, mumbling phrases which he neither feels nor understands. Expression of this kind still has no meaning even when he puts together a number of phrases to form a sentence because the original causation of the statement is merely aped without an original plan or design through which the meaning can be expressed.

The lack of order and design in most works is due partly to a lack of creative attitude (too much dependence or emphasis on nature) and partly to ignorance of the basic laws of plastic unity. These two ideas are almost interchangeable. If the imitative "artist" were convinced of the virtue of being creative, he would probably be helpless without nature to lean on. Many liberal-minded artists today find themselves in this predicament.

If they lack the character or ability to get down to the hard toil of searching out and learning to use the fundamentals of creative design and plastic unity,

FIGURE 126. Woman with White Gloves, by Cecilia Beaux. A weak, naturalistic portrait, with emphasis placed on tricky brush strokes and general slickness. With exception of upper part of head, picture is almost devoid of form or design. Compare with Figure 127. (Collection, Whitney Museum of American Art.)

by whether or not a picture is pretty enough to be placed over the mantel in the front parlor. This attitude has been nurtured both by painters, who find it a more pleasant means of making a living than through sincere toil, and by picture dealers with more commercial interest than aesthetic idealism.

Most painters are perhaps unaware of a lack of subtlety and taste in their work. At least, we would assume this from the fact that even in their most serious noncommercial works their taste is little better. This lack of taste is most clearly found in the use of color —in calendarlike pictures that are all sirup and saccharin, with mountain peaks in the sunset which catch bright orange highlights and the shadows colored a brilliant purple or violet; or fields of daffodils and sweet bluebonnets. This is a style of painting like the stories of sweetness and light in a love pulp at the corner drug store. This sugary depiction of the trite and obvious is almost always carried by a weak and squishy form.

Imagination is one of the most important attributes of the artistic mind. Without it there can be little of creation, expressive meaning, or originality; with it they either end up by imitating shallow surface effects of genuine creative works or fall back into naturalistic imitation with some face-saving opinion like, "there's nothing to this crazy new stuff—it's just a passing fad." In a great many cases, by the time an artist sees the light it is too late to change because of lifelong habits of nature imitation.

Most pictures are just that, merely pictures. They have nothing in particular to say to the mind or the spirit—nothing special, other than the trite and obvious that has already been said so many countless times that it has become hackneyed and meaningless. Not necessarily that the subject must be new, but certainly the vision must, or else the whole business of art is no more than a ritual.

Many painters of a popular ilk have learned the tricks of the painting craft very well indeed—so well, that they have learned to say nothing very cleverly. This superficial technique is taken by many to be a superior product. The lay public has been led to believe that art is judged by sweet sentimentality and

FIGURE 127. Concetta, by Ernest Fiene. Compare the technical simplicity and design quality of this picture with Figure 126. (Collection, Whitney Museum. Photograph, courtesy, Associated American Artists, Inc.)

one is able to reach beyond the ordinary, creating powerful reality out of the merest obscurity, making the most fantastic convincingly real.

It takes courage as well as natural ability to be original. Originality is most usually misunderstood and criticized by those having little of it themselves. To be original is to be unconventional and abnormal to some degree, to be different from the average run of men. This distinctiveness sets one apart, and a person possessing it is taken as being peculiar and eccentric. As a result many painters, writers, composers, and other artists of real individuality are considered to be just a little crazy. It takes courage to be original and individualistic under these circumstances.

FIGURE 128. Landscape, by Edward Redfield. An example of squishy painting, impressionistic copying of surface facts. If work of this kind has any value, it is sentimental and descriptive, not plastic. Note lack of simplification and order in details of foreground shrubbery, trees, and hills. Sky is left blank, making a large hole in back plane, thus violating the closed-field principle. Compare with Figures 92 and 101. (*Courtesy, Whitney Museum of American Art.*)

The character and philosophy of the artist as an individual must be directly related to his work; or rather the converse, his work must be a direct expression of nature or imagination as experienced by him.

To one who is familiar with such things, the whole character of an artist can be read in his work. It can be seen whether the man is honest, sincere, sensitive, stupid, realistic, romantic, imaginative, visionary, deep, superficial, clumsy, clever, individualistic, strong, serious, humorous, or countless other things.

The lack of originality to be found in most works might be said to exist because of a lack of originality in the artists themselves, or lack of the kind of courage it takes to be individualistic in spite of misunderstanding and ridicule.

Lack of originality is directly related to lack of creativeness in that copying or imitating nature is an impersonal craft that leaves little room for expression of original forms or moods.

Most pieces have a smattering of creativeness, order, meaning, taste, and even originality, but only rarely are these attributes emphasized enough for one piece to become something uncommon, personal, complete, and fine—in short, a genuinely good work of art.

Now to reiterate concerning unity—unity and consistency in technique, style, form, and expression. Within the range of creative art there are many possible ways of working. There is realism, in which the outward appearances of nature are retained. There is abstraction, in which certain natural objects are redesigned into symbols that represent these things. There is semiabstraction, in which natural appearances are moderately abstracted for purposes of design or expression.

There is decoration, in which sensuous aspects of design, color, and texture are emphasized. There is surrealism, in which ideas and impressions of the subconscious mind are depicted. There are impressionism, expressionism, pointillism, nonobjectivism, and cubism. There are many more forms of the past and present as well as those yet to be invented in the future. It is for each individual to find his own means of expression, not by copying or imitating the work of any artist or school, ancient or modern, but by arriving at a personal philosophy consistent with his own time and place, and developing an original technique and form by which it can best be expressed.

Whatever this form might be, the measuring gauges for quality are creativeness and unity. A work will have quality if there is consistency in style and technique, form and theme, spirit and function. Such a new creative organism exists in its own right as any other creation in nature exists—bound into a living oneness by the principles of unity.

12. PRACTICE THEORY

The list of practice exercises following this chapter is made up as a complete course, beginning with simple exercises concentrating on a single means in relation to an isolated principle of unity, then working toward a complete orchestration of all the means and all the principles of form, theme, and technique in conjunction. Where time does not permit working out the full course, several of the lessons might be combined into one exercise, such as in unity of line where some or all of the problems under this heading may be combined into one or two experiments. However, where time does permit, the lessons can be learned more thoroughly by separating each step, giving plenty of time for thought and digestion of each.

The course is made up especially for the painter, but most of the design problems are the same for sculptor, architect, applied artist, and the rest; and the lessons might be learned by following them as outlined or applying them to any other specific medium. The course closely follows the subjects as they are outlined in this book so that the student may study the text along with each problem given, then analyze and criticize the results accordingly.

To attain a well-rounded knowledge of design, both the feelings and the intellect must be exercised and developed. The relative amount of each in the synthesis is a moot question and must be answered according to the needs of each personality. However, it is true that most of us have an inborn sense of beauty and rightness which will lend individuality, feeling, and unity to a work if it is encouraged to assert itself in the creating. Accordingly the emphasis should be placed rather on the side of the intuitive, bringing out this talent in each student, subordinating the lessons of rule and mind to a position of secondary importance—as kinds of introductory exercises, suggesting the underlying principles by which the emotions may be guided.

Some artists find it a good method to do many free, emotional preliminary sketches, either small or large, then selecting the most promising of these for the finished work; others work out the design directly on canvas. By experimenting, one can decide which works better for himself, and learn the advantages and disadvantages of each. Sometimes in the former method in transferring the sketch to the canvas, much of the free spontaneity of the original is lost. In the latter method there is a tendency to be fearful of wasting good materials, which hampers free expression. A compromise between the two ways may be used, making preliminary sketches but leaving part of the perfecting and finishing to be done directly on the canvas.

After the conscious rule is once thoroughly learned through theory and practice, it may then be forgotten and all the work thereafter done basically by intuitive means. Where time is no object, each of the lessons outlined may be followed with emotional practice of the principles involved in each case.

As for materials, these need not be of a costly nature, especially during the early part of the course. The paper may be some medium-weight pencil or charcoal variety about twenty by twenty-two inches in size. Where easels are available, students should use these and after tacking paper onto drawing boards, stand at work in order to ensure freedom of action. The drawing may be done in charcoal, which shows up well and is easy to erase when necessary. When charcoal drawings are done that one wants to preserve, they may be sprayed with a commercial fixative or white shellac thinned with alcohol.

For the exercises in color, ordinary poster or gouache colors will do, and where a group is working together, these may be purchased in pint or quart jars. A large water-color brush (No. 12) and a soft half-inch housepainter's or artist's bristle brush will do for the most part. When students get into advanced experiments, they will want to work with better materials of all sorts. By this time they will have had enough experience to know just what they need and where to purchase the same.

For advanced work a good set of sable water-color brushes should be used, a large wash brush and two or three smaller ones of various sizes, medium, smaller, and extra small; also, a fairly good grade of water-color paper. For advanced work (or even early work for that matter) a set of gouache or water colors may be hand ground by the students, using a formula from one of the books on technique listed at the end of the book. A suggested simple palette coinciding with that of the professional artist would be the following: yellow ochre, cadmium yellow, burnt sienna, burnt umber, cadmium red-light, ultramarine blue, ivory black, emeraude or veridian green, and zinc white or titanium white.

Reproductions of paintings, sculpture, architecture, applied arts, and the rest are a good source for study and are necessary for the lessons on analysis.

For the analytical problems reproductions of paintings found in books or magazines are best to use. An ordinary soft-lead pencil will do. Tracing paper is used for this and is placed over the reproduction being studied, the lines, spaces, or other parts being traced directly on the paper which may be tacked down so it will remain stationary. When analyzing color, crayons or colored pencils may be used. These analytical studies may be done best perhaps with students sitting at tables.

Where time permits, special days may be set out for studies in analysis. Otherwise, a part of each lesson period, preferably before experimenting on the study of the moment, may be used, so students may become thoroughly acquainted with the problem before the creative practice of it. There is one danger here that the student must beware of, and that is a tendency to imitate the work or method of the artist whose work he has just analyzed. This may be overcome by using the principle involved but substituting totally different subject matter from that analyzed. Being aware of this danger and working from basic principles, there should be no trouble in bringing out the creative in each individual.

Most of the practice lessons may be matched by periods of analysis of reproductions on each problem involved. Periods of analysis and discussion of later and more advanced problems may be had without using tracing paper, merely setting up large reproductions or original art works when available. Group visits to museums and art exhibits are an important means of interest and learning.

While complete freedom in choice of style or approach should be allowed, for the sake of developing the creative nature, the abstract rather than the realistic should be emphasized in all the practice experiments up to the final advanced ones. Free use of arbitrary design, color, symbolism, and distortion should be encouraged.

When or if the student does come to work realistically, he should be careful to retain the creative approach, redesigning and reorganizing nature, rather than slipping back into a noncreative, imitative way of doing. When realistic subject matter is used, it is well to look at the work from the abstract point of view. A help is occasionally to turn the picture upside down for analysis, even working on it in this position at times. Another way is to hold it up to a mirror, which reverses the design and shows up flaws that might have gone unnoticed.

Because color is rather complex in nature, the different aspects of it, where unity is concerned, are separated and made into individual exercises. While it is unnecessary for an artist to go into details of the scientific aspects of color, it is wise to learn certain basic things about the subject. One should know from memory the colors of the twelve- and twenty-four color circle, the complement of each hue, the difference between the pigmentary and light spectrums, how to gray a color, how to make a tint and a shade, the various types of color harmony and contrast, and so on.

The first consideration in all the experiments, analytical or otherwise, is the frame lines within which the picture is to be arranged. Before each problem is begun, the boundary should be clearly decided and marked out, for every line and color placed on the paper should be in relation to this format.

In all the exercises, creative or analytical, major things should come first. The large masses, lines, and other means should be blocked in before the secondary ones. Each added line, tone, volume, or color should be placed in felt relation to the rest. Unless otherwise stated, all exercises are to be drawn from imagination or memory in order to develop the creative powers.

The most insistent fault of beginners is to become engrossed in detail, forgetting the large masses and their relation to the whole. In drawing from the human figure, most of them will labor over a head, a leg, or an arm before deciding, even in their mind's eye, whether the whole figure is correctly designed in relation to the format, or whether the larger parts harmonize with each other or the whole.

In order to attain in early exercises the greatest interest and variety of pattern contour and to develop a way of better seeing and controlling the space patterns in the whole design, it is useful for the student

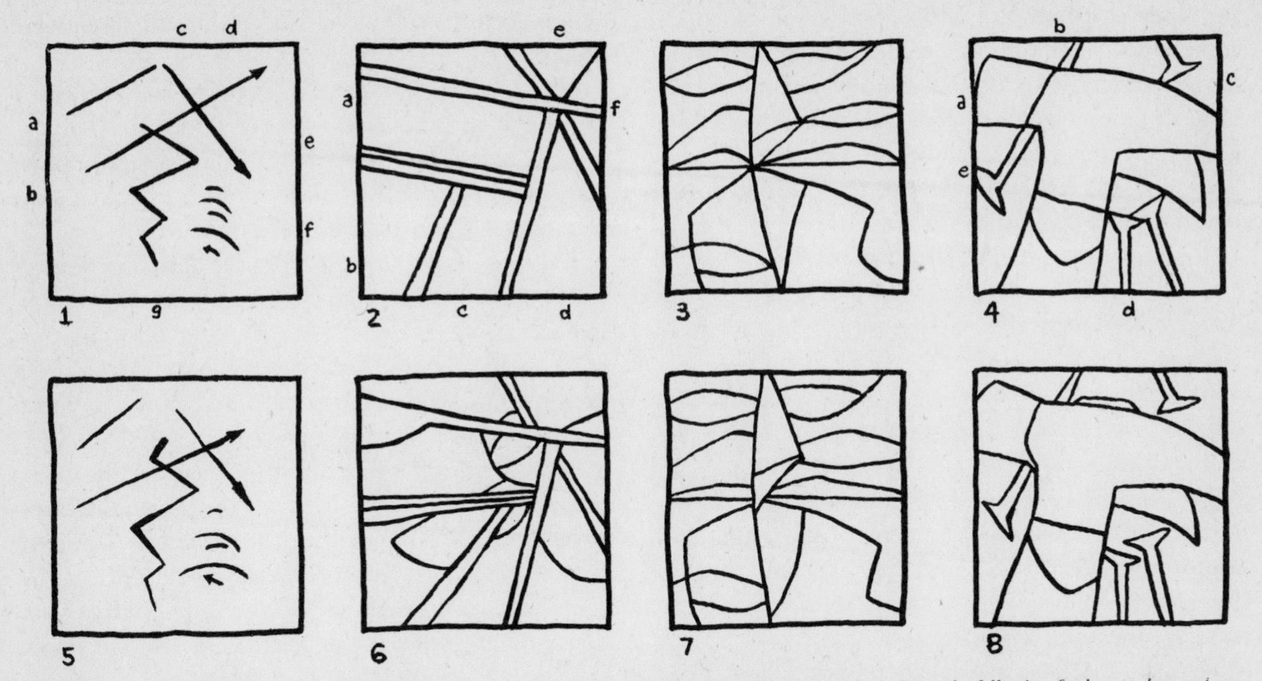

FIGURE 129. Ill-arranged and corrected designs. In 1 there is an arbitrary line arrangement which shows the following faults: top-heavy, large lines too near the top of frame, too much space around the bottom. Lines a and b and horizontal position of zig-zag line too much in same direction. Line a too close to arrow c. Spaces directly below c and d and opposite e from tips of arrows to their crossing and from this point to the left, have distances too much the same, creating a static point. Curved lines at f monotonous in direction and size. Zig-zag line g badly proportioned and lacking in transition at the top end, relative to nearby lines. In design 5 these faults are corrected, and in addition lines are given variety by heavier accents at some points. 2 shows an arbitrary line-space arrangement which shows the following faults: Space areas at a, b, c, d, and e are too monotonously alike. The lines that make up these spaces are too repetitious in direction and unrelated to the essential shape of the frame at the left side and bottom. (No transition around the corners.) Static points at upper right-hand corner and where lines cross at e and f. Line f too nearly centered between corner and diagonal line below at the right. Center of interest created by crosslines e and f too far out of pictorial center. In 6 these faults are corrected. Also extra space patterns are added to contrast with straight lines and help throw more weight down toward the left. While this does not exactly make a perfect design, a comparison of the two will show the improvement. In 3 is seen an arbitrary space arrangement in which static points are used as part of the motif, showing that rules may be broken if the artist makes it an obvious and consistent part of the design, and, of course, if he is clever enough to make it work. In this case nearly all the patterns touch the frame or each other. 7 shows how the design is harmed rather than improved by eliminating several of these static points, although there is some improvement in the space proportions. In 4 is shown a space-subject arrangement with the following faults: Horizontal line at a converges with frame too abruptly. Upright line at end of hammer shows the other extreme. It goes too much in the same direction as the frame line, creating a static point where the two lines meet the frame. Diagonal line of nail and crossline on hammer come together, creating a static point. Other static points are found at c, d, and e. In 8 all these faults have been corrected. An extra space was added on top of the hammer to repeat the several nailhead shapes in the lower half of the design.

to keep all or most of the patterns closed until the final phase of the work. This is an important point, because by doing this the student will get into the habit of considering every area for pattern variation in the single units, and the single patterns in relation to the whole.

Simplicity should be the objective in all first exercises, limiting the student to a few elements of line, space, color, or volume. Then gradually they develop more complexity as he attains greater power and mastery of organization. Debates and discussions of books on each subject, as it is taken up, add interest and variety to the course. Subjects may be assigned from the supplementary reading list with the addition of any other available material. Musical recordings or dramatic stories are good means of setting the mood before, or during, the exercises on theme and expression.

A method that develops self-reliance and objective thinking, as well as giving each student an opportunity to take advantage of the mistakes of others where several are working on the same problem, is to set up all the work in front of the room and invite free criticism from each student in turn, with the instructor as chairman, filling in with pertinent questions and conclusions.

After each exercise is finished and set up for criticism, some general questions, which fit the particular case, may be asked:

Is it a personal expression? Is it creative? Is it too intellectualized? Does it show emotional freedom? Is it too stiff, tight, academic? Is it unified? Where have the rules of unity been broken? Could it be improved by adding anything? Subtracting? Does it possess variety in all its parts? Is there enough contrast? Is there a rhythmic relationship

1
2
3
4
5
6
7
8
9

throughout? Are there static points or areas that could be relieved? Is there transition around the corners? Are certain elements repeated often enough?

In line arrangements, are remaining spaces varied in size and shape? Do some lines or masses crowd the frame too much at some points? Are there dominant masses and subordinate ones? Or are there too many elements of the same strength clashing or fighting each other? Are the major elements near enough to the center of the picture, or are they so near to the frame lines as to throw the whole off balance?

Are both positive and negative space patterns unusual and interesting in shape? Are distance planes placed in good sequence and balance in all three dimensions? Is there a focal point or center of interest? Do directional planes have rhythmic and oppositional relationship in their arrangement? Do colors, tones, and textures integrate to set planes in right positions in distance and direction? Or do some colors, tones, textures, planes, or volumes seem to "jump" out of their correct position in the three-dimensional field?

Is the field completely unified and closed? Where subject matter is used, is it integrated with design? Does it express the mood and feeling intended? Where rules have been broken, has the artist gotten away with it?

These are only some of the most usual questions to be asked and answered. There are many others which may be pertinent to the problem at hand, many of which are suggested in the text and illustrations of this book.

FIGURE 131. Peruvian Textile (detail). A design based on line and pattern opposition. (Collection, Metropolitan Museum of Art.)

FIGURE 130. (on facing page) Light-dark analysis of various paintings in from three to five tones. 1. The Calmady Children, by Sir Thomas Lawrence, English, 1880. A poor arrangement of tone values in that lights in the two figures are conglomerated, confused in pattern, allowing of no consistent eye movement through the whole. 2. The Wyndham Sisters, by John S. Sargent, American, 1900. Picture divided too equally between light and dark. Lower half cluttered and lacking in tone variation. Repetition of some definite patterns of light in the upper half and dark in the lower half would help tie the two halves together. 3. The Annunciation, by Aelbrecht Bouts, Dutch, about 1500. A fine integration of subject and design. Figures attract main interest by being strongest in light-dark contrast against a medium light background. All tones clearly defined and repeated throughout. 4. The Honorable Frances Duncombe, by Thomas Gainsborough, about 1775. A fair arrangement of tones spoiled by confused light patterns around the hands of the figure and in the background nearby. Also, light in upper left-hand corner too strong. 5. Rinaldo and Armida, by Anthony Van Dyck, about 1625. Tones scattered and cut up. Poor relationship in proportions of tone masses. Each figure and object so cut up in light-dark that it is hard to make out the subjects. 6 Panic, by Abraham Rattner, contemporary American. A complex but well-integrated organization of tone values arranged on a two-dimensional plane. 7. Sunday on the Reefs, by Marsden Hartley, contemporary American. Structurally solid and straight to the point. Fine adjustment of tone spaces. 8. The Two Lovers, by an unknown German, about 1580. Tones used simply and decoratively to make for a pleasing and well-organized design. 9. Two Women, by Diego Rivera, contemporary Mexican. Bigness and strength through stark simplicity. A contrast of white and black against a medium-toned background. Tone spaces perfectly thought out and designed.

13. PRACTICE EXERCISES*

UNITY OF LINE (Text, page 16, Refs. 12, 13, 17)

1. Opposition

After drawing a number of frames four or five inches wide on a full sheet of paper, fill each with a nonobjective (without subject) arrangement of straight lines in opposing directions, lengths, and other characteristics. In order to keep strictly within the problem of line, none of them should touch each other or the frame in a way that would create enclosed spaces (Fig. 132 *A* and *B*).

2. Transition

Draw boundary frames as in No. 1. Within each frame design an arbitrary line arrangement using a limited number (say three to five) straight lines in various directions, emphasizing the principles of rhythm and repetition (Fig. 132 *C* and *D*).

3. Opposition and Transition

Within boundary frames as in Nos. 1 and 2, draw straight- and curved-line designs without subject, combining the principles of opposition and transition (Fig. 132 *E* to *H*).

4. Complete Unity of Line

After dividing a full sheet of paper into two large frames, fill each with a nonobjective line design, combining all the principles of unity—rhythm, repetition, opposition, dominance, and variation, using lines of different width, tone, and character.

* Numbers at the beginning of each new group of exercises refer to the text on each subject, and to bibliographical references listed in the back of the book, which will aid in solving the problems.

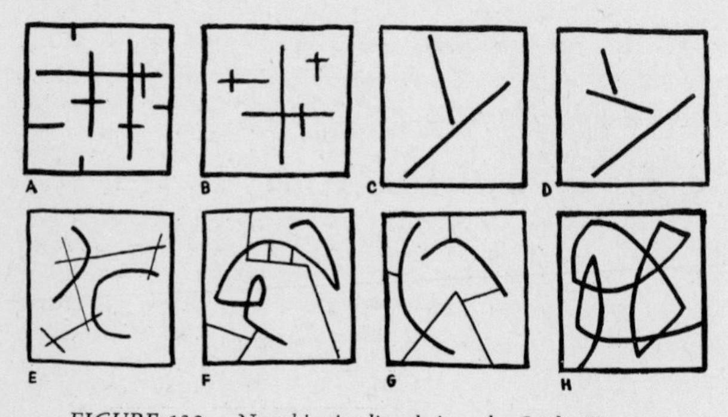

FIGURE 132. Nonobjective line designs, by Gaylen Hansen.

5. Line Unity plus Subject

Draw one large boundary frame, using full-sized sheet of paper. Design a semiabstract line arrangement combining subject matter. Suggested subjects: (*a*) Simple landscape consisting of hills, clouds, trees, and road. (*b*) Potato pickers in field—rows of furrows, potato bags, trees and hills added in background. (*c*) Horses or other animals, close up or in landscape. (*d*) Still life.

UNITY OF PATTERN (TWO-DIMENSIONAL SPACE) (Text, page 17, Refs. 12, 13, 14, 18)

6. Opposition

After drawing frames as in No. 1, using a limited number of horizontal and vertical straight lines, fill with nonobjective pattern designs by making lines touch each other or the frame, leaving spaces in good oppositional arrangement (Fig. 134 *A*, *B*, and *C*).

FIGURE 133. Panel from States of the Mind, by Boccioni. Free use of rhythmic line within the framed field. (Collection, Museum of Modern Art.)

FIGURE 134. Nonobjective two-dimensional space designs.

FIGURE 135. Garden in Soichi, by Arshile Gorky. (Collection, Museum of Modern Art.)

7. *Pattern, Opposition, and Transition*

(*a*) After drawing frames, using a limited number of straight lines, fill with nonobjective designs as seen in Fig. 134 *D*.

(*b*) Same as (*a*), using curved or curved and straight lines (Fig. 134 *E* and *F*).

8. *Complete Unity of Pattern*

Within frames as in No. 1, draw nonobjective pattern designs, using both straight and curved lines, combining transition, opposition, domination, and variation of size, shape, and general character (Fig. 134 *G* and *H*).

9. *Pattern-Contour Variation*

Using full sheet of paper and disregarding structural design for the moment, create many types of space shapes that are unusual and varied, emphasizing free emotional approach (Fig. 29 *B*).

10. *Pattern-Contour Variation plus Unity*

After drawing frames nearly full size of paper, make unified nonobjective designs with varied contour spaces (Fig. 135). Other interesting experiments in this exercise and No. 9 may be carried out by cutting various pattern shapes out of cardboard or paper, then assembling them with pins or paste on a simple background, working for variation and unity. As a first experiment, one approach is to divide the whole area into varied spaces with a few straight and curved lines, similar to exercise No. 8, and later develop the areas into interesting pattern shapes.

11. *Pattern Variation plus Subject*

Using full sheets of paper and disregarding structural design for the moment, create interesting contour patterns of single natural objects. Suggested subjects: (*a*) Landscape motifs—tree, mountain, cloud, house, and shrubbery. (*b*) People, animals, or parts of their anatomies—heads, hands, feet, and the like. (*c*) Still-life objects—fruit, vegetables, baskets, bowls, dishes, flowers, drapery, and so on (Fig. 136).

12. *Pattern Unity plus Subject*

Using a full sheet of paper, create seventy-five-percent abstract designs, combining pattern with subject matter in a unified way. Suggested subjects: (*a*) Objects or people seen around the workroom. (*b*) Still life —flowers, table, cloth, books, or other things. (*c*) Fish and other aquatic creatures. (*d*) The stage with dancers moving across it.

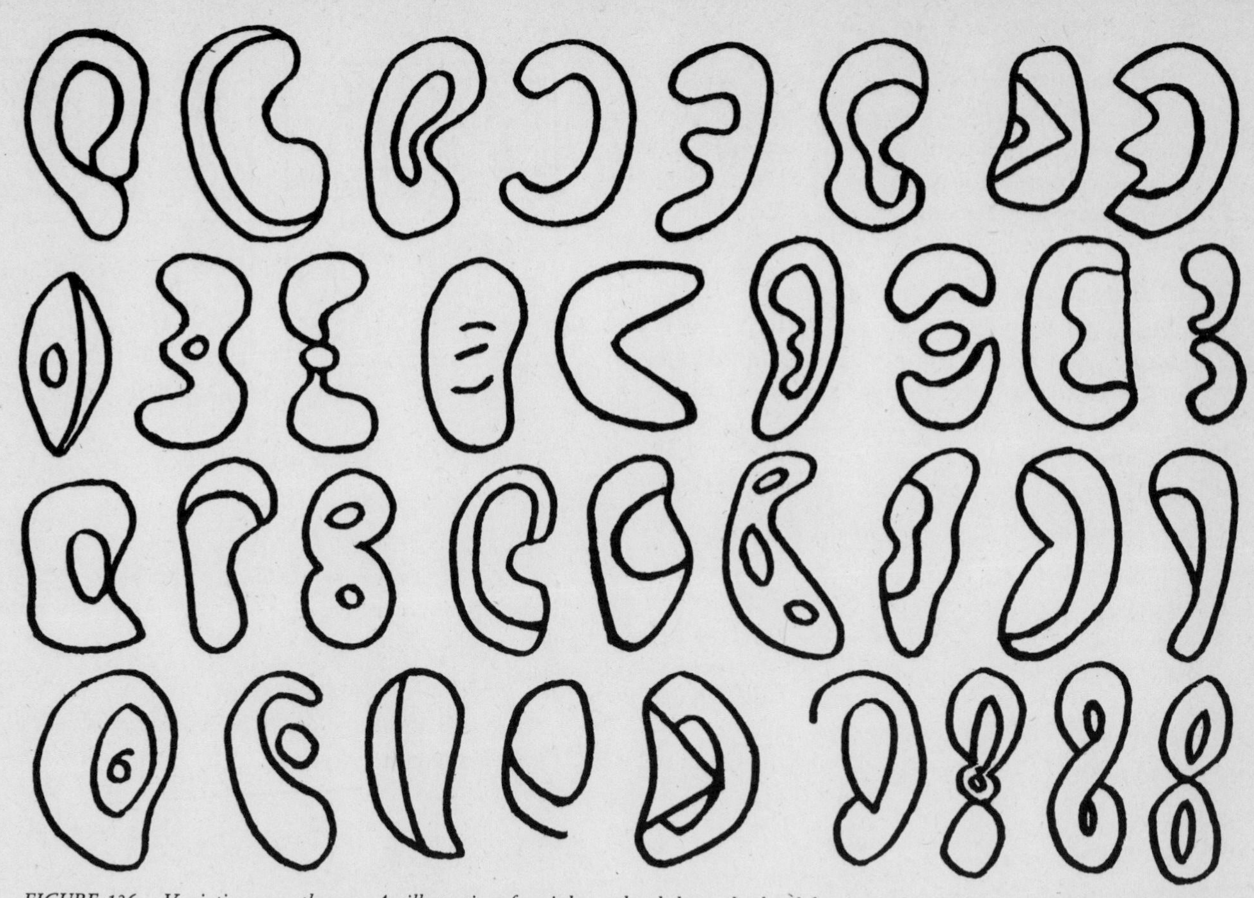

FIGURE 136. Variations on a theme. An illustration of varied yet related shapes developed from a single motif; in this instance, the human ear.

UNITY OF TONE (Text, page 19, Refs. 12, 13, 16)

13. Emotional Tone Exercise

Using full sheets of paper and black and white poster colors, make free-emotional tone designs without subject, directly and without preliminary drawing. While the general principles of unity might be remembered, the point here is to develop a spirit of freedom and play with tones, feeling rather than thinking out good arrangements, sequences, and contrasts, and developing a sense of rightness by intuition rather than intellectual calculation.

14. Opposition

After creating nonobjective pattern design within half-sheet-size formats, fill in with balanced arrangement of complementary tones—black and white or any two on opposite sides of a neutral medium tone. Either charcoal or poster colors may be used, keeping to flat, two-dimensional patterns.

15. Transition

After creating nonobjective pattern design about three-fourths-size of full sheet, fill in with limited number of tones (say three to five) in analogous relationship.

16. Complete Unity of Tone

After creating nonobjective space design on full or three-fourths-size sheet of paper, fill in with tones in full unity, emphasizing rhythm, repetition, opposition, variation, and domination.

17. Tone Unity plus Subject

Keeping all the principles in mind from past lessons, create a semiabstract pattern-tone design combining subject matter. Suggested subjects: (*a*) City landscape—buildings, streets, vehicles, people, and the like. (*b*) People at work—laborers, craftsmen, office workers, and so on. (*c*) Sports—football, baseball, tennis, swimming, and such.

UNITY OF COLOR (Text, page 20, Refs. 19 to 21)

18. Emotional Color Exercise (Ref. 11)

Using full sheets of paper and red, yellow, and blue gouache or poster paints, and forgetting design principles for the moment, fill the paper with color harmonies, chords, and contrasts that are pleasing to the individual tastes and feelings. Play with the color. Smear and blend the two or three primaries together on the paper to form rhythms and contrasts that seem right because they arouse the emotions in some way. Be direct. Do not muddy the colors by working over. Sense the beauties of color. Forget technique. Be a child again. Have fun.

19. Opposition of Hue

Using a half sheet of paper and one color plus one complement, work directly without preliminary drawing and make a balanced design of spots, squares, or various pattern shapes, illustrating the principle of hue contrast.

20. Opposition of Intensity and Hue

Using a half sheet of paper and two colors plus one mutual complement, each in a different intensity, work directly without preliminary drawing to make a balanced design of spots, squares, or patterns, illustrating the principles of hue and intensity contrast. (A color is grayed by adding a little of its complement or black.)

21. Opposition of Hue, Intensity, and Tone

Using half sheets of paper and three colors plus two mutual complements, each in different intensity with the colors in contrasting tone value to the complements, without preliminary drawing make a balanced arrangement of spots, squares, or patterns, illustrating the principle of tone, hue, and intensity contrast. (Colors are lightened by adding white or a lighter hue and darkened by adding a darker hue or black.)

FIGURE 137. *Subject-space arrangements, by Shirley.*

22. Rhythm of Hue

Using a half sheet of paper and three or four analogous colors, without preliminary drawing make an interesting nonobjective space arrangement, illustrating the principle of rhythmic color.

23. Rhythm of Hue and Intensity

Using a half sheet of paper and five to seven analogous hues in rhythmic sequence of intensity, without pre-

FIGURE 138. *The Chessboard, by Juan Gris. Natural subject abstracted and organized into an interesting arrangement of patterns, tone values, and lines. (Collection, Museum of Modern Art.)*

FIGURE 139. *Student abstract and semiabstract space-tone designs.* (*Art Department, University of Texas.*)

liminary drawing make an interesting nonobjective space arrangement, illustrating the principles of rhythmic hue and intensity. (If using hues from a twelve-color circle or less, no more than six should be used in the sequence, because a seventh color would be over the line on the complementary half of the circle. However, using smaller steps, as in a twenty-four-hue circle, any number up to twelve may be used.)

24. Rhythm of Hue, Intensity, and Tone

Using a half sheet of paper and five to seven analogous hues in rhythmic sequence of intensity and tone, without preliminary drawing make an interesting nonobjective space and line arrangement, illustrating the principles of rhythmic hue, intensity, and tone.

25. Complete Unity of Color

(*a*) Using a half sheet of paper and five to seven analogous hues in rhythmic sequence of intensity and tone, plus two mutual complements, without preliminary drawing make an interesting nonobjective space and line arrangement, combining all the principles of color unity thus far considered.

(*b*) Other exercises using subject matter.

FIGURE 140. The Prodigal Son, by Max Beckmann. (Collection, Museum of Modern Art.)

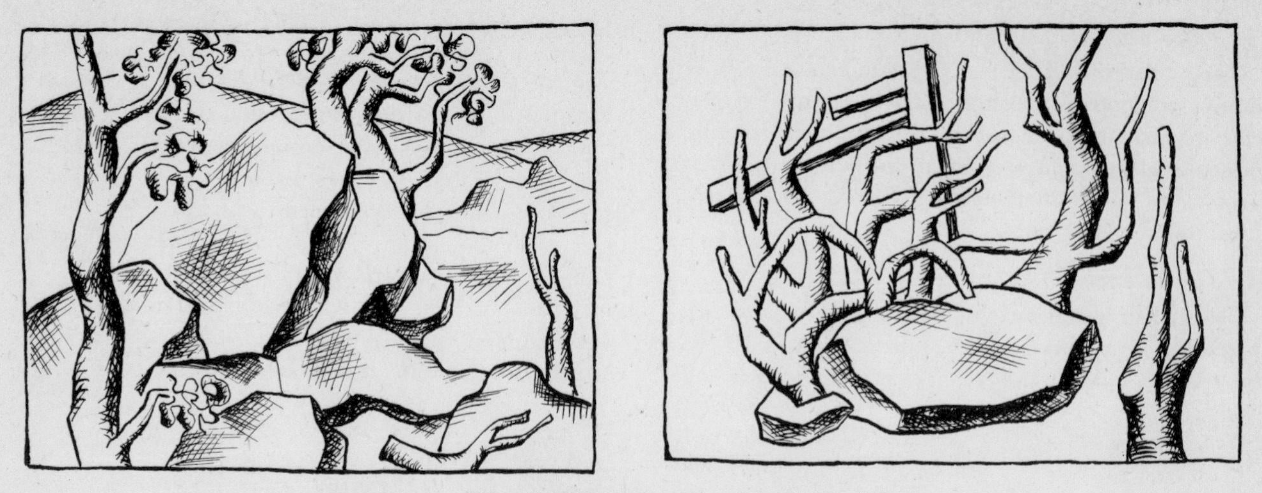

FIGURE 141. Three-dimensional space-subject designs by Frank Bacher.

UNITY OF TEXTURE (Text, page 23, Refs. 63, 67)

26. Texture Experiments

Using a full sheet of paper, divide into a number of interesting enclosed-space patterns. Disregarding design for the moment, fill each space with a different variety of texture, using any hues, intensities, or tones desired. Lines, dots, washes, cross hatchings, spatters, stipples, glazes, rhythms, contrasts, thick paint, thin paint—these are suggestions of textures the student might invent. Different tools like tooth brush, comb, razor blade, burlap, or sponge may be tried in the experiment.

27. Complete Unity of Texture

Using a full sheet of paper, without preliminary drawing make a nonobjective space and line design, emphasizing varied textures in relation to the laws of unity.

28. Unity of Line, Pattern, Tone, Color, and Texture

Using a full sheet of paper, with or without preliminary drawing, design a nonobjective picture comprising all the means and principles of unity taken up thus far.

FIGURE 142. Composition with Tree, by Gaylen Hansen. Decorative textures made with various types of lines.

29. Line, Pattern, Tone, Color, and Texture plus Subject

Using a full sheet of paper, with or without preliminary drawing, design a modified realistic picture comprising all the means and principles of unity plus subject. Suggested subjects: (*a*) Circus life—animals, clowns, tents, laborers, wagons, and so on. (*b*) Children at play. (*c*) Artists or craftsmen at work. (*d*) Political struggle and strife.

THIRD-DIMENSION EXERCISES (Text, page 24, Refs. 22 to 27)

30. Third-dimensional Line

After drawing a number of frames eight or ten inches wide on a full sheet of paper, using charcoal or pencil, fill each with an abstract or semiabstract design, emphasizing third-dimensional line. (Recessional thrusts and movements by means of line perspective, overlapping, and rhythms.)

31. Third-dimensional Space

After drawing a number of frames as in No. 30 with pencil or charcoal, fill each with a simple abstract or semiabstract design stressing third-dimensional space. (Backward-forward movements and balances by means of free perspective, overlapping, and so on.)

32. Third-dimensional Tone

After drawing a number of frames eight or ten inches wide, with charcoal, pencil, crayon, or black-and-white paints, fill each with an abstract or semiabstract design, stressing third-dimensional light-dark values. Make some pictures in shallow recession, others in deep space. (Third-dimensional movements and balances by means of receding-advancing tone, overlapping edges, and so on.)

33. *Third-dimensional Color*

Using a half or full sheet of paper and colors, with or without preliminary drawing, make a seventy-five-percent abstract or semiabstract design, experimenting with color planes. (Third-dimensional movements and balances by means of receding-advancing hues, intensities, tones, and so on.)

34. *Third-dimensional Texture*

Using a half or full sheet of paper and colors, make an abstract or semiabstract design, experimenting with texture planes. (Backward and forward movements and balances created by means of loud or quiet textures.)

35. *Volume Organization* (*Text page* 35)

Using half or full sheets of paper and charcoal or pencil, create some nonobjective designs with three-dimensional volumes (cubes, cones, cylinders, pyramids, or spheres) in unified three-dimensional space arrangements. Do the same exercise plus subject. Suggested subjects: (*a*) Indoor objects—chairs, tables, boxes, and so on. (*b*) City landscape—buildings, streets, bridges, traffic, and the like. (*c*) Factory life—workers, trucks, barrels, boxes, crates, and so on.

FIGURE 143. Head of a Woman, by Pablo Picasso. Natural subject abstracted in terms of cubic planes. (Collection Paul Guillaume, Paris. Photograph, courtesy, Museum of Modern Art.)

36. Directional Plane Organization

Using half or full sheets of paper and charcoal or pencil, create nonobjective arrangements of varied directional planes in unified three-dimensional space. Do the same exercise plus subject. See No. 35 for suggested subjects. Also: (*a*) Still life—ceiling, floor, chair, table, objects on table like books, jewelry box, vase, and the like. (*b*) Large cubistic head. (*c*) Cubistic full figure.

37. Unity of the Total Means

Using full sheets of paper, and with preliminary drawing in pencil or charcoal, create nonobjective designs in color, incorporating all the means, space, line, tone, color, texture, volumes, and planes in three dimensions. Do the same exercise plus subject. Suggested subjects: (*a*) Still life—flowers, table, drapery, and the like. (*b*) Orchestra playing. (*c*) Musical instruments in still life. (*d*) People at work or play. Other pictures may be developed from nature—posed models, landscape, etc.

THEME AND EXPRESSION (Text, page 56, Refs. 31 to 33)

38. Expressive Symbolism

Using half or full sheets of paper and charcoal, create abstract and semiabstract designs symbolizing various moods like tranquillity, stability, happiness, hate, fear, love, jealousy, or others.

39. Expressive Symbolism plus Color

Using half or full sheets of paper, without preliminary drawing create abstract and semiabstract designs in color, depicting moods different from those in No. 38.

40. Expressive Symbolism plus Subject

Using full sheets of paper and charcoal, momentarily disregarding design, fill with single semiabstract natural objects, distorting or changing their appearance to express certain moods. Suggested subjects: trees, flowers, furniture, still-life objects, people, and so on.

FIGURE 144. *Wild Horses, by Cecil Smith.*

FIGURE 145. *Driftwood, by Everett Spruce. (Courtesy, the artist.)*

41. Unity of Total Means plus Theme and Expression

Using full sheets of paper, and with preliminary drawing in charcoal or pencil, create abstract, semiabstract, and realistic designs incorporating all the means, line, tone, space, color, texture, expressive symbolism, and theme in unified three-dimensional arrangements. Suggested subjects: fire, pestilence, flood, death, war, earthquake, crucifixion, spring, winter, and so on.

TECHNIQUE (Text, page 69, Refs. 11)

42. Broken Color (Text, page 71)

After drawing a number of frames four or five inches wide on a full sheet of paper, fill each with one of the following broken-color experiments: (*a*) Using primary colors, cover whole white area with red and yellow dots in correct proportions, the end result equaling vermilion. (*b*) Using primaries yellow and blue, the end result equaling violet. (*d*) Using primary yellow and secondary vermilion, the end result equaling orange. (*e*) Do the same with other primaries and secondaries. (*f*) Do the same with a little of the mutual complement added. (*g*) Try similar experiments with grayed colors.

43. Free-broken Color with Subject

Using full sheets of paper and any or all of the six primary and secondary colors, create unified designs with subject, using broken color in free-emotional manner (Fig. 96).

ADVANCED EXPERIMENTS (Refs. 34 to 45)

44. Experiments with Various Media

Using good quality materials, experiment with various

media—oils, pastels, water colors, tempera, and others, developing a knowledge of and sensitivity to intrinsic qualities of each. Many of the problems already studied may be used but handled in a more advanced, serious way.

45. *Tactile Experiments* (*Refs.* 63, 67)

Using various materials of different textural qualities, make charts and serious abstract designs that are interesting to the sight and touch. Suggested materials: sand, pebbles, buttons, glass, screen wire, paint, plaster, cardboard, wood, paper, fur, leather, tin, velvet, silk, wool, tacks, wallpaper, and so on.

46. *Various Techniques* (*Refs.* 34 *to* 36)

Make serious paintings using various technical methods, such as glazing, scumbling, direct opaque, varnish, tempera, gouache, and others.

47. *Form Exercises* (*Ref.* 36)

Suggested projects: (*a*) After designing a good arrangement of two-dimensional patterns, with or without subject, fill in with arbitrary colors in flat, medium tones. Then draw out forms in a more or less bas-relief fashion by highlighting one side and shading the other of the pattern contours. (*b*) Do the same as in (*a*) but model the forms by drawing out the lights and darks on the interior of the patterns, developing full three-dimensional forms. (*c*) Do the same as in (*b*), but draw out lights in soft shading at the center of each form, later accenting edges with darks. (Front planes—those closest to the spectator—are those to be drawn out with lights.) (*d*) Begin with flat-color patterns in light tones, then develop form by working toward the darks. (This is a good procedure for working in a transparent medium such as water color.) (*e*) Begin with patterns in darkest tones, develop form by working toward the lights. (*f*) Invent other methods and techniques for developing form. (*g*) Do other pictures developed from nature.

FIGURE 147. Blue Morning, by Emlen Etting. (Courtesy, Midtown Galleries.)

FIGURE 146. Of Domestic Utility, by Charles Sheeler. (Collection, Museum of Modern Art.)

48. *Various Palettes* (*Ref.* 37)

Make serious paintings, some developed from nature, in each using a different palette of colors from which a simplified color scheme may be mixed. Suggested palettes: (*a*) Zinc white, yellow ochre, light red, and ultramarine blue. (*b*) Zinc white, yellow ochre, burnt sienna, and ivory black (the black to take the place of blue, by mixing with white). (*c*) Zinc white, cadmium yellow, cadmium red-medium, and cobalt blue. (*d*) Zinc white, yellow ochre, Venetian red or Indian red, ultramarine blue, and lamp black. (*e*) Zinc white, raw sienna, cadmium red, alizarin crimson, and ivory black. Many other simplified combinations may be used to suit the individual need and taste.

49. *Set Palettes* (*Ref.* 10)

Make serious paintings, some developed from nature, in each using a different set palette. (This consists of deciding a general color scheme and premixing most or all of the colors before starting to paint, setting them out on the palette, and applying them directly to the canvas, later making any necessary modifications or additions.)

50. *Tonal Color*

Make paintings taken from nature, in each using a different set palette with all the colors modified with a tonal color: (*a*) Yellow. (*b*) Green. (*c*) Blue. (*d*) Red.

FIGURE 148. Phippsburg, Maine—1932, by John Marin. (Courtesy, An American Place.)

FIGURE 149. Summer Landscape, by Stuart Davis. A semiabstraction of a natural scene. Compare with Figure 150. (Collection, Museum of Modern Art.)

FIGURE 150. Landscape in Colors of a Pear, by Stuart Davis. Same subject as Figure 149, further abstracted. (Collection, Cranbrook Academy of Art.)

MEMORY AND CREATIVE PRACTICE (Refs. 48, 55)

51. Creative Interpretation

Working from life, landscape, still life, or photograph, redesign into abstract or semiabstract arrangements in black and white or color.

52. Transposed Design

Working from reproductions of paintings or photographs, on full or half sheets of paper, analyze line and space structure. Then put reproduction aside and create a new picture within the lines and spaces (different subject from that analyzed).

CREATIVE FIGURE EXERCISES (Refs. 11, 27, 28, 29, 55)

53. Geometric Figures

On a full sheet of paper design a nude figure, using geometric forms in place of realistic ones (cylinders, cubes, cones, spheres, and the like). In this exercise action and volume arrangement is the aim. If a model is used, students may avoid static poses by having him go through motions of a given action, rather than holding a set pose.

54. Rhythmic Line

Using a model, make a semiabstract design, accentuating rhythmic lines, keeping forms big and simple. Add background lines to complete composition.

55. Semiabstract Interpretation

Using model (nature, landscape, still life, or human) as a motif, make semiabstract designs with simple, flat, geometric patterns such as squares, circles, rectangles, and triangles.

56. Memory and Creative Practice

Using a nude or draped model, create a picture in designed realism, working with back turned or in another room from model. Do the same with still life and other subjects, some in black and white, some in color.

57. Transposed Views

Working from life or reproductions of figure photographs or paintings, create a drawing, showing figure from side not seen. (If figure in reproduction is seen from the front, draw from imagination the pose as it would look from the back, and so on.)

58. Transposed Perspective

Working from life or reproductions, make designs with perspective transposed. (If seen from above, draw from the side or below, and so on.)

59. Projects

Advanced projects may be carried out, with several students and sometimes instructor collaborating, such as murals, sculpture, stage scenery, interior decoration, year book, and many others to fit the needs of school, home, or public institution.

BIBLIOGRAPHY

THE CREATIVE ATTITUDE AND THE ARTIST'S PROBLEM

Theory

1. *Art and Education*, by Dewey, Buermyer, and others—Barnes Foundation Press.
2. *Art as Experience*, by John Dewey—Minton, Balch & Co.
3. *The Artist Sees Differently*, by Duncan Phillips—E. Weyhe.
4. *The Creative Adult*, by Hughes Mearns—Doubleday, Doran & Company, Inc.
5. *The Mind in the Making*, by James Harvey Robinson—Harper & Brothers.
6. *Primer of Modern Art*, by Sheldon Cheney—Tudor Publishing Company.
7. *Theory and the Substance of Art*, by Louis W. Flaccus—F. S. Crofts & Co.
8. *What Is Modern Painting*, by Alfred Barr, Jr.—Museum of Modern Art.

Practice

9. *The Arts in the Classroom*, by Natalie Cole— John Day Company.
10. *The Art Spirit*, by Robert Henri—J. B. Lippincott Company.
11. *The New Art Education*, by Ralph M. Pearson—Harper & Brothers.

UNITY OF THE MEANS

General

12. *Art for Amateurs and Students*, by George Cox—Doubleday, Page & Company.
13. *Composition*, by Arthur W. Dow—Doubleday, Doran & Company, Inc.
14. *Dynamic Symmetry*, by Jay Hambidge—Yale University Press.
15. *Experiencing Pictures*, by Ralph M. Pearson—Brewer, Warren & Putnam.
16. *Painting for Beginners*, by Jan Gordon—Garden City Publishing Company, Inc.
17. *Practice of Drawing*, by Harold Speed—Seeley, Service & Co., Ltd.

Color

18. *Color Science*, by Wilhelm Ostwald—Winsor & Newton, Ltd.
19. *The Art of Color and Design*, by Maitland Graves—McGraw-Hill Book Company, Inc.
20. *The Enjoyment and Use of Color*, by Walter Sargent—Charles Scribner's Sons.
21. *The Study of Color*, by Michel Jacobs—Doubleday, Doran & Company, Inc.

THE THIRD DIMENSION AND THE TOTAL MEANS

22. *The Art in Painting*, by Albert C. Barnes—Harcourt, Brace & Company, Inc.
23. *The Art of Cézanne*, by Albert C. Barnes—Harcourt, Brace & Company, Inc.
24. *Cézanne's Composition*, by Erle Loran—University of Calfornia Press.
25. *Expressionism in Art*, by Sheldon Cheney—Liveright Publishing Corp.
26. *The Language of Vision*, by Gyorgy Kepes—Paul Theobald Co.
27. *The Problem of Form*, by Hildebrand—G. E. Stechert & Company.

THEME AND EXPRESSION

The Human Figure

28. *Art and the Life*, by Geo. J. Cox—Doubleday, Page & Company.
29. *An Atlas of Anatomy for Artists*, by Fritz Schider—Dover Publications, Inc.
30. *The Natural Way to Draw*, by Kimon Nicolaides—Houghton Mifflin Company.

Color

31. *The Art of Color*, by Michel Jacobs—Doubleday, Doran & Company, Inc.
32. *The Functions of Color in Painting*, by Duncan Phillips and C. Law Watkins—Phillips Memorial Gallery.
33. *The Language of Design*, by C. Law Watkins—Phillips Memorial Gallery.

TECHNIQUE

General

34. *Encyclopaedia Britannica* (Sections on Art Crafts and Techniques).
35. *The Artist's Handbook of Materials and Techniques*, by Ralph Mayer—The Viking Press, Inc.

36. *The Materials of the Artist and Their Use in Painting*, by Max Doerner—Harcourt, Brace & Company, Inc.

37. *Notes on the Technique of Painting*, by Hilaire Hiler—Oxford University Press.

Special Media

38. *How I Make Woodcuts and Engravings*, by Hans Mueller—American Artists Group.

39. *Making a Lithograph*, by Stow Wengenroth—The Studio Publications, Inc.

40. *Making an Etching*, by Levon West—The Studio Publications, Inc.

41. *Making Watercolor Behave*, by Eliot O'Hara—Minton, Balch & Co.

42. *The Practice of Tempera Painting*, by Daniel V. Thompson, Jr.—Yale University Press.

43. *Zorach Explains Sculpture*, by William Zorach—American Artists Group.

44. *Silk Screen as a Fine Art*, by J. I. Biegeleisen—McGraw-Hill Book Company, Inc.

45. *The Technique of Watercclor Painting*, by Richmond & Littlejohns—Sir Isaac Pitman & Sons, Ltd.

PAINTING AND SCULPTURE

General

46. *Abstract and Surrealist Art in America*, by Sidney Janis—Reynal & Hitchcock, Inc.

47. *The Art and Craft of Drawing*, by Vernon Blake—Oxford University Press.

48. *Cubism and Abstract Art*, by Alfred Barr, Jr.—Museum of Modern Art.

49. *Experiencing American Paintings*, by Ralph M. Pearson—Harper & Brothers.

50. *The Gist of Art*, by John Sloan—American Artists Group.

51. *The Meaning of Modern Sculpture*, by R. H. Wilenski—Frederick A. Stokes Company.

52. *Paul Cézanne*, by Gerstle Mack—Alfred A. Knopf, Inc.

53. *Painting for Pleasure*, by Morris Davidson—Hale, Cushman & Flint.

54. *Personal Revolution and Picasso*, by Louis Danz—Longmans, Green & Co., Inc.

55. *Picasso—Forty Years of His Art*, by Alfred Barr, Jr.—Museum of Modern Art.

56. *Plastic and Pure Plastic Art*, by Piet Mondrian—Wittenborn, Schultz, Inc.

57. *Representation and Form*, by Walter Abell—Charles Scribner's Sons.

58. *Why Abstract?*, by Hilaire Hiler—New Directions.

FUNCTIONAL DESIGN AND ART IN EVERY-DAY USE

59. *Art and Industry*, by Herbert Read—Harcourt, Brace & Company, Inc.

60. *Art and the Machine*, by Sheldon and Martha Cheney—The Viking Press, Inc.

61. *Art in Everyday Life*, by Goldstein and Goldstein—The Macmillan Company.

62. *Art Today*, by Faulkner, Ziegfeld, and Hill—Henry Holt & Company, Inc.

63. *Bauhaus*, 1919–1928, by Bayer, Gropius, and Gropius—Museum of Modern Art.

64. *Design This Day*, by Walter Dorwin Teague—Harcourt, Brace & Company, Inc.

65. *Good-bye, Mr. Chippendale*, by T. H. Robsjohn-Gibbings—Alfred A. Knopf, Inc.

66. *Industrial Design*, by Harold Van Doren—McGraw-Hill Book Company, Inc.

67. *The New Vision*, by L. Moholy-Nagy—Wittenborn, Schultz, Inc.

Art History

68. *Art in the Western World*, by Robb and Garrison—Harper & Brothers.

69. *Art Through the Ages*, by Helen Gardner—Harcourt, Brace & Company, Inc.

70. *History of Architecture on a Comparative Basis*, by Bannister Fletcher—Charles Scribner's Sons.

71. *History of Art*, by Elie Faure—Harper & Brothers.

72. *The Arts and Man*, by Raymond Stites—McGraw-Hill Book Company, Inc.

73. *The Story of Modern Art*, by Sheldon Cheney—The Viking Press, Inc.

74. *World History of Art*, by Sheldon Cheney—The Viking Press, Inc.

ART MAGAZINES

75. *American Artist*. Monthly. New York.

76. *The Art Digest*. Semimonthly, October to May, inclusive; monthly, June, July, August, and September. New York.

77. *Art News*. Monthly. New York.

78. *Magazine of Art*. Monthly. October through May. Washington, D. C.

INDEX

U

V